The Power of Pentecost

The Power of Pentecost

An Examination of Acts 2:17–21

MARTIN C. SALTER

RESOURCE *Publications* • Eugene, Oregon

THE POWER OF PENTECOST
An Examination of Acts 2:17–21

Copyright © 2012 Martin C. Salter. All rights reserved. Except for brief quotations in critical publications or reviews, no part of this book may be reproduced in any manner without prior written permission from the publisher. Write: Permissions, Wipf and Stock Publishers, 199 W. 8th Ave., Suite 3, Eugene, OR 97401.

Resource Publications
An Imprint of Wipf and Stock Publishers
199 W. 8th Ave., Suite 3
Eugene, OR 97401
www.wipfandstock.com

ISBN 13: 978-1-61097-248-2

Manufactured in the U.S.A.

All scripture quotations, unless otherwise indicated, are taken from the Holy Bible, New International Version®, NIV®. Copyright ©1973, 1978, 1984 by Biblica, Inc.™ Used by permission of Zondervan. All rights reserved worldwide.

For Sarah, Noah, Abigail, and Keziah

καὶ ἔσται πᾶς ὃς ἂν ἐπικαλέσηται τὸ ὄνομα κυρίου σωθήσεται.

Contents

Foreword ix
Preface xi
Acknowledgments xiii
Abbreviations list xv
Introduction xix

1 An Exegesis of Acts 2:17–21 • 1

2 Acts 2:17–21 within the context of Acts 1–2 • 21

3 Acts 2:17–21 within the subsequent narrative of Acts • 39

4 Acts 2:17–21 within Luke's overall purpose • 59

5 Acts 2:17–21 in contemporary debate • 76

Conclusion 97
Bibliography 101

Foreword

THE PERSON and work of the Holy Spirit is essential for the existence of the pastor-theologian but is also a challenge for such a hyphenated role. Of course, all and every gift to the churches is, in some way, an enabling by the Spirit, but the breadth of the Spirit's dynamic presence also stretches the hyphen even as it enables it. On one side of the hyphen, the pastor works with real people in real situations, and might well be tempted to minister according to mere memory or pragmatism instead of from an ongoing reading of the Spirit's variegated works across scripture. On the hyphen's other face, the theologian all too often tends towards exegeting at a distance, abstracted from the particularities inherent within daily and perennial lived experience of the local church. To be a pastor-theologian is an ongoing art, a craft replete with tension and opportunity. It is a gift to such people and their churches when a writer helps strengthen the connection between pastor and theologian; it is a gift of the Spirit.

I'm pleased and honoured to introduce this volume by Martin Salter, as one which will nourish the pastor-theologian and will also highlight the author as an exemplar of this hyphenated craft. In the pages which follow, a wide spread of scholarship relating to the Spirit in Acts is distilled and evaluated. This alone is a great service to both theologian and pastor. At the same time, and arising from this careful exegetical work, Martin Salter also leads us to an insightful and thoughtful consideration of how the Spirit's portrayal in Acts impinges on the life of churches seeking to live today within his illumination and empowerment. Furthermore, in all this, there are many helpful pointers towards how we can best read biblical narrative theologically, with a consistent attention to its narrative form. Too many pastors

Foreword

feel an unease in this important reading skill, as also do not a few theologians, and here is a book which will model an approach to a responsible and grounded narrative-theological reading.

I'm confident in commending this book, having known Martin Salter in both the classroom and in ministry situations, and having seen him working out these pages in both reflection and practice. This volume has arisen out of a Masters dissertation of the highest standard, and out of teaching Acts to both adults and young people in various settings. The Keswick Youth Convention, an annual event held in the Lake District town of that name in the United Kingdom, has benefited greatly from Martin's teaching and training over the past few years, and he is now establishing himself as an insightful young local church minister within the independent evangelical church scene within the UK. Having supervised his Masters research, in many ways I hope Martin gains the opportunity to move on to doctoral studies, but I know either the academy or the local church will benefit from his involvement. And, with an eye to that hyphenated role of pastor-theologian, may he continue to manage to bridge both poles. This book is testimony to an ability to connect both these spheres and, as such, I wish it a wide readership and anticipate it being a help to many.

Here is thoughtful engagement for those who would consider themselves charismatic, for those who would eschew such a label, and for those who are unsure or—more importantly—want to read and think and live beyond the all-too-easy shorthand that labels can announce. The debate surrounding matter of the Spirit's work within the churches will be greatly helped by each and every chapter of this work. It is not the last word on the topic, but it is a very calm and considered way-marker. In the same way, I hope it is not the last published work from Martin Salter, but a first fruits of more to come.

Revd. Dr. Matthew Sleeman
Oak Hill College
London

Advent 2011

Preface

THE SUBJECT of this book reflects a long term interest in charismatic issues and debate, and arises out of a thesis undertaken at theological college on this subject. Personally, I come from a background of conservative evangelical churches, and having friends in other traditions has stimulated me toward further exploration of these issues. Of particular interest, is the relationship between the more extraordinary phenomena seen in the early church, and the absence of such things (at least in practice) in many of the churches with which I am most familiar. This work has enabled me to wrestle more deeply with some of these issues and I am grateful for that opportunity. The subject of the book itself is obviously limited and to that end I am not here supposing that I will make the definitive contribution to a significant and wide-ranging debate. If this work can make a small contribution to the ongoing discussion then that will be sufficient.

Acknowledgments

I wish to say a huge thank you to all those who helped to make this book possible. What began as an MTh dissertation, has, thanks to much encouragement from others, become what it is. Thank you to Oak Hill College for four wonderful years of training and then permitting me two weeks last summer to use the library and write. Thank you especially to Dr. Matthew Sleeman without whose supervision, insightful critique, and constant guidance, this book would never have become a reality. Thanks also to my loving family who allowed me time to study, put me up, and put up with me in the process. Many thanks to all those who read drafts and offered constructive comment: Jim Murkett, Mark Ventham, Phil Sweeting, Ray Evans, and Bill James.

The ultimate word of thanks must go the Holy Spirit who enabled me to write any truth contained herein. The errors are all mine!

Sola Dei Gloria

Abbreviations

AB	Anchor Bible
ABD	*The Anchor Bible Dictionary.* 6 vols. Edited by David Noel Freedman. New York: Doubleday, 1992
ANF	Ante-Nicene Fathers
ANTC	Abingdon New Testament Commentaries
BAIIFCS	Book of Acts in Its First Century Setting
BDAG	Walter Bauer, Frederick W. Danker, W. F. Arndt, and F. W. Gingrich. *Greek-English Lexicon of the New Testament and Other Early Christian Literature.* 3rd ed. Chicago: University of Chicago Press, 2000
BDF	Friedrich Blass, and Albert Debrunner. *A Greek Grammar of the New Testament and Other Early Christian Literature.* Translated and revised by Robert W. Funk. Chicago: University of Chicago Press, 1961
BECNT	Baker Exegetical Commentary on the New Testament
BI	Biblical Interpretation
BST	The Bible Speaks Today
BNTC	Black's New Testament Commentaries
BTB	Biblical Theology Bulletin
BTCB	Brazos Theological Commentary on the Bible
BZNW	Beihefte zur Zeitschrift für die nuetestamentliche Wissenschaft

Abbreviations

CBQ	*Catholic Biblical Quarterly*
CCT	*Contours of Christian Theology Series*
EBC	*Expositor's Bible Commentary*
EDNT	*Exegetical Dictionary of the New Testament*. Edited by Horst Balz and Gerhard Schneider. Grand Rapids: Eerdmans, 1991
EQ	*Evangelical Quarterly*
ESV	*English Standard Version*
GNT	*Greek New Testament*
HALOT	*Hebrew and Aramaic Lexicon of the Old Testament.*
HTR	*Harvard Theological Review*
IBS	*Irish Biblical Studies*
ICC	*International Critical Commentary*
IVPNTC	*InterVarsity Press New Testament Commentary*
JBL	*Journal of Biblical Literature*
JETS	*Journal of the Evangelical Theological Society*
JPT	*Journal for Pentecostal Theology*
JPTSup	*Journal of Pentecostal Theology: Supplement Series*
JSNTSup	*Journal for the Study of the New Testament: Supplement Series*
JTS	*Journal of Theological Studies*
L&N	*Greek-English Lexicon of the New Testament: Based on Semantic Domains*. Edited by J.P.Louw and E.A. Nida. 2nd ed. New York, 1989
LCC	*Library of Christian Classics*
LCL	*Loeb Classical Library*
LHD	*Library of History and Doctrine*
LNTS	*Library of New Testament Studies*

LSJ	Liddell, H.G., R. Scott, H.S. Jones. *A Greek-English Lexicon*. 9th ed.
LXX	Septuagint
MT	Masoretic Text
NAC	New American Commentary
NBD	*New Bible Dictionary*. Edited by I. H. Marshall et al. Leicester, 1996
NIB	New Interpreter's Bible
NICNT	New International Commentary on the New Testament
NIDNTT	*New International Dictionary of New Testament Theology*. 4 vols. Edited by C. Brown. Grand Rapids: Eerdmans, 1975–85
NIDOTTE	*New International Dictionary of Old Testament Theology and Exegesis*. 5 vols. Edited by Willem A. Van Gemeren. Grand Rapids: Zondervan, 2008
NIGTC	New International Greek Testament Commentary
NIVAC	New International Version Application Commentary
NovT	Novum Testamentum
NovTSup	Supplements to Novum Testamentum
NPNF	Nicene and Post-Nicene Fathers
NTC	New Testament Commentaries
NTL	New Testament Library
NTM	New Testament Monographs
NTS	New Testament Studies
PCNT	Paideia Commentaries on the New Testament
PNTC	Pillar New Testament Commentary
SBB	Stuttgarter Biblische Beiträge

Abbreviations

SBG	Studies in Biblical Greek
SBLDS	Society of Biblical Literature Dissertation Series
SBLMS	Society of Biblical Literature Monograph Series
SBT	Studies in Biblical Theology
SNTSMS	Society for New Testament Studies Monograph Series
SP	Sacra Pagina
TDNT	Theological Dictionary of the New Testament. 10 vols. Edited by Gerhard Kittel and Gerhard Friedrich. Translated by Geoffrey W. Bromiley. Grand Rapids: Eerdmans, 1964–76
TNIV	Today's New International Version
TNTC	Tyndale New Testament Commentary
TynB	Tyndale Bulletin
UBS	United Bible Societies Greek New Testament (4th ed.)
VE	Vox Evangelica
WBC	Word Biblical Commentary
WTJ	Westminster Theological Journal
WUNT	Wissenschaftliche Untersuchungen zum Neuen Testament
ZNW	Zeitschrift für die Neuetestamentiche Wissenschaft

Introduction

ALMOST 2000 years ago a Jewish fisherman stood up with eleven friends to address a great multitude in Jerusalem at the feast of Pentecost. The crowd present had heard an uneducated group of Galileans declaring the wonders of God in a plethora of different languages. Peter's explanation? This was what had been foretold by the prophet Joel—a divine promise to pour out the Holy Spirit on all flesh; a promise that sons and daughters would prophesy; that young men would see visions, and old men dream dreams; that signs and wonders would be manifest. This was a promise from God for all his people throughout the last days. It was, and remains, a truly extraordinary promise. The question is what do we, as twenty-first century Christians, make of the promise?

In the ongoing debates over the charismatic use of spiritual gifts, the book of Acts is often cited. Scholars arguing for a continuationist position note how frequently tongues, prophecy, and miracles occur, and argue such things are normative for the church today.[1] Conservative scholars, on the other hand, argue that such phenomena in Acts serve a particular revelatory function at a particular point in redemptive history and should not, therefore, be considered normative.[2]

The text of Acts 2:17-21 is *crux interpretum* in the debate. MacArthur goes so far as to say "without question, the second

---

1. For example Deere, *Surprised By The Voice of God*, 60-63; Green, *I Believe in the Holy Spirit*, 16; Keener, *Gift and Giver*, 95-97; Oss, "Pentecostal/Charismatic," 267; Wagner, *The Third Wave*, 1-5; Wimber, *Power Evangelism*, 116-117.

2. See MacArthur, *Charismatic Chaos*, 217; Stott, *Baptism and Fullness*, 28-30; Gaffin, *Perspectives on Pentecost*, 14-22; Palmer Robertson, *The Final Word*, 58, 60.

Introduction

chapter of Acts is *the key passage* of Scripture from which Pentecostals and charismatics develop their theology."[3] It is key, not least, because it is seen by many as a programmatic text for the rest of the narrative,[4] and by some as a programmatic text for the church more widely.[5] This crucial text, therefore, raises a number of questions: are the promises contained therein for a particular generation; for every Christian; or do they still await complete fulfilment? If they are for every Christian what exactly will that look like for the twenty-first century church? Will it look the same globally or will cultural factors dictate? Is fervency of expectation or intensity of faith a factor?

The implications of the answers to such questions are significant for contemporary church practice. Acts scholar, Max Turner, commenting on Acts 2:16–39 notes:

> It would quite literally be nonsense to suggest the writer of Luke-Acts *anticipated* the cessation of these: if indeed they ceased, such a state of affairs could only have come as a considerable surprise to him. It would inevitably have seemed like a failure at the very heart of what Joel's promise of the Spirit was all about.[6]

At the opposite end of the spectrum MacArthur states:

> Some Bible teachers say that Peter was pointing to Pentecost as a fulfilment of Joel 2:28. But on the day of Pentecost there were no wonders in the heavens and signs in the earth; no blood and fire and vapors of smoke; the sun did not turn to darkness and the moon to blood and the great and terrible day of the Lord did not come. The prophecy was not fully realized;

---

3. MacArthur, *Charismatic Chaos,* 212. Emphasis mine.

4. For example Tannehill, *The Narrative Unity of Luke-Acts* 2, 29; Turner, *Power From On High,* 267.

5. Menzies, "Acts 2:17–21: A Paradigm for Pentecostal Mission," 200–218.

6. Turner, *The Holy Spirit and Spiritual Gifts,* 298. Emphasis original.

Introduction

> Pentecost was only a partial fulfilment, or better, a preview of the prophecy's ultimate culmination.[7]

Thus, for MacArthur, the phenomena described by Joel are still awaiting future fulfilment; tongues-speech and prophesy have no place in the contemporary practice of the church. We can begin to see the importance of Acts 2:17–21 within the debates. As we understand this great prophecy in its original context, in the context of Peter's speech, and in the wider context of the narrative of Acts, we will hopefully begin to understand what it means and what it looks like for this prophecy to be fulfilled.

To that end, this book will examine the text on multiple levels. In chapter 1 we will exegete the quotation as it stands in Acts 2:17–21, considering the various textual changes from the Septuagint of Joel 2:28–32 (3:1–5 LXX). We shall be able to gain some preliminary understanding as to the meaning and relationships of its various words and clauses. In chapter 2 we shall look at the prophecy in the context of Acts 1–2, arguing that the restoration of Israel in her new exodus is a key Lucan theme. In so far as that is the case, the events of Pentecost must be seen as climactic and constitutive of the prophetic hope for a restored community indwelt by the Spirit. In chapter 3 we shall examine how the prophecy is fulfilled and functions within the wider narrative of Acts. Many of the phenomena mentioned in Acts 2:17–21 reappear through the narrative of Acts. This examination will provide, not only a greater understanding of what those phenomena look like and how Luke understands them, but also a clearer appreciation of their purpose and function. In chapter 4 we shall consider the contribution of the passage as regards Luke's literary endeavour. We shall be exploring wider questions such as Luke's purpose and how his portrayal of the Holy Spirit serves his rhetorical ends. This is important in beginning to address how to determine what elements of Luke's narrative are intended as normative. In chapter 5 we will begin to cross the bridge towards the contemporary de-

---

7. MacArthur, *Charismatic Chaos*, 288.

Introduction

bates, examining the various positions, and how the investigation presented addresses the questions and issues commonly raised. Finally, we shall pull together the threads of the argument and draw some conclusions.

Let me here give a word about methodology. It may seem to put the cart before the horse to examine the text before the context. Why not begin with Luke's purpose and then home in on the text in question in ever more focused concentric circles? In reply, it should be said that to approach the text that way would necessitate a full-scale Lucan theology which would warrant a multi-volume work in itself—something that is well beyond this author's resources of talent or time. Further, it would take so long to get to the subject matter of this book that even the most patient reader would have probably put it to the bottom of the bed-time reading pile. The approach adopted here will be more like building up a picture in a series of layers. At each stage of enquiry we shall gain a slightly clearer and richer picture of how to understand the text and think about applying it to our own situations.

The aim is to engage with and incorporate the best insights of the various contributors within the debates. The thesis is thus twofold. First, Luke presents his story as the climax of Israel's story[8]—the pouring out of the Spirit is for the restoration of Israel in her new exodus.[9] Thus there is something uniquely significant about Pentecost as a climactic moment. However, and secondly,

---

8. Wright, *The New Testament and the People of God*, 378–84.

9. This is argued for at length by Turner, *Power*, 267–315, 418–27. See also Ravens, *Luke and the Restoration of Israel*, 215; Pao, *Acts and the Isaianic New Exodus*. Pao particularly picks up on the new exodus theme in Isaiah 40–55 noting thematic parallels to Acts and the linguistic connections between the "way" language in Isaiah (דרך—40:3; 43:19; 51:10) and in Acts (ὁδός—19:9, 23; 22:4; 24:14, 22). The restoration of Israel is part of this new exodus, and this restoration includes reconstitution of "Israel", ingathering of exiles, the community of the Spirit, rebuilding the Davidic kingdom, repentance, and inclusion of outcasts. See Pao, *Acts*, 51–69; 111–76. All of these themes are present in Acts as Luke presents the restoration of Israel in her new exodus. This conceptual context will be important in considering Acts 2:17–21.

Introduction

Pentecost (and its out-workings) does provide a promissory pattern of what this renewed Israel will look like—a family portrait—which will include the "empowerment to witness"[10] described in the terms of Acts 2:17–21, and fleshed out in the subsequent narrative. The details will have to await the discussion of subsequent chapters, but these are the twin theses for which I shall be arguing.

The discussions are often as fierce as they are important. Are some churches leading people astray, falsely claiming divine guidance, disrupting good order, and harming the flock in their application of texts like Acts 2:17–21? Or are other churches quenching the Spirit, refusing to listen, and closing eyes and ears to the guidance and blessing of God? Such issues are seldom black and white; real life is lived in the grey, but what can be seen is that, for the good of the flock, pastors need clearly thought through answers, rooted in good exegesis of Scripture, as they approach and engage with this particular theological hot potato. In my own experience this promise, or at least its more miraculous elements, are too frequently explained away or glossed over. For others, from a more Pentecostal or charismatic tradition, some elements within the promise are claimed as a paradigm for Christian salvation and/or practice in every place and age. As Poythress notes, "the critics of the charismatic movement are tempted to be indiscriminating. But so are its advocates. The easy, blunt, self-confident answer, "the movement is *all* of God" is unbiblical, just as is its reverse, "It is all a delusion.""[11] The hope is that this book may, in some small way, contribute a little less heat and a little more light to an issue of great contemporary importance. I do not claim it will in any sense be the last word—rather the continuation of a conversation.

---

10. Empowerment to witness as a distinctively Lucan emphasis is argued for by Menzies, *Empowered for Witness*, 47–49; E. Schweizer, "πνεῦμα," 404–415.

11. Poythress, "Linguistic and Sociological Analyses," 489.

1

An Exegesis of Acts 2:17–21

INTRODUCTION

THE OBVIOUS place to begin this study is the text itself of Acts 2:17–21. In subsequent chapters we shall move to consider the wider context as well as the narrative fulfilment of these verses within Acts, but first a close examination of the verses themselves is in order.

In this chapter we will examine the verses in terms of their syntactic and logical relationships, as well as beginning to address some of the interpretative issues. Of particular interest here are the changes made in Acts 2:17–21 to the LXX and MT of Joel 3:1–5, and the significance of those changes. The literary context will very briefly be given but will be explored more fully in subsequent chapters.

LITERARY CONTEXT

At the start of Acts Luke narrates the risen Christ's final meetings with his disciples (1:3–8) prior to his ascension into heaven. In Acts 1:8 the disciples are told to remain in Jerusalem and await the promised Holy Spirit which will empower them to be Jesus' witnesses in Jerusalem, Judea and Samaria, and ultimately to the ends of the earth. After Christ has ascended (1:9–11) and the replacement for Judas has been decided (1:23–26) we arrive at the

THE POWER OF PENTECOST

start of Acts 2 in anticipation of the promise being fulfilled. The promised Holy Spirit descends as the 120 disciples are gathered together (2:1; cf. 1:15), and phenomena like flames of fire, wind, and speaking in other languages are heard to the wonderment of the Pentecost crowd. In 2:14 Peter stands to address the crowd and explain the events just witnessed. His speech contains three Old Testament quotes (Joel 3:1–5; Ps 16:8–11; 110:1) culminating in an appeal to repent and be baptized. Luke tells us that three thousand converts were added to the believing community that day (Acts 2:41). The citation of Joel 3:1–5 in Acts 2:17–21 is in response to the crowd's amazement at the events witnessed, and it is the content and meaning of these verses which now warrants our attention.

EXEGESIS OF ACTS 2:17–21

I propose to examine the quotation phrase by phrase addressing pertinent questions along the way. Following the *refutatio* regarding revelry of v. 15, Peter's opening in v. 16 is a good example of *pesher* exegesis under the "this is that" formula.[1] Peter contends that the phenomena experienced and witnessed by those present occur as part of the fulfilment of those things about which Joel's prophecy spoke.[2]

Verse 17

καὶ ἔσται ἐν ταῖς ἐσχάταις ἡμέραις λέγει ὁ θεός
(And it will be, in the last days, God says)[3]

---

1. Longenecker, *Biblical Exegesis in the Apostolic Period*, 83; Alexander, ""This is That": The Authority of Scripture in The Acts of the Apostles," 61; Parsons, *Acts*, 42.

2. Although Codex D and Irenaeus lack a reference to Joel, its inclusion is far better attested, and given the content of the quotation it is clearly a reference to Joel 3:1–5 (LXX). Bock, *Proclamation From Prophecy and Pattern*, 158.

3. My own somewhat wooden translations will be included here for the benefit of the reader who does not read NT Greek.

An Exegesis of Acts 2:17-21

Peter begins by citing something which the prophet Joel saw as future, as indicated by his use of the future indicative verb, εἰμι (to be). Peter, however, alters the wording of Joel 3:1 as it appears in the LXX where it reads καὶ ἔσται μετὰ ταῦτα (and it will be after these things). This is the first of six changes from the LXX in Peter's citation.[4] Peter moves away from the more general μετὰ ταῦτα (after these things) to the more redemptively significant ἐν ταῖς ἐσχάταις ἡμέραις (in the last days).[5]

A key question immediately raised is to what do these "last days" refer? Some scholars have made the case that the "last days" refers to the period running up to and culminating in Jerusalem's destruction in AD 70, based upon a preterist understanding of the signs in the sun and moon mentioned in Acts 2:19.[6] These signs will be considered in more detail below. Here we need to take note of four other NT references to "the last days". The same phrase occurs in 2 Tim 3:1; Heb 1:2; Jam 5:3; 2 Pet 3:3. The first three of these references could plausibly take a preterist interpretation (that is the primary reference of the prophecy is AD 70), but the fourth, 2 Peter 3:1-13, cannot. Read in context (2 Pet 3:1-13) the reference is clearly to the age culminating in the "new heavens and new earth" (2 Pet 3:13). Therefore, while a preterist reading is possible, it can only be partial—it cannot exhaust the scope of "the last days". It seems preferable to take "the last days" as referring to the entire period up until the coming of the "new heavens and new earth."[7] Crucially for this study, these words place the Pentecost event within God's final stage of redemption, a stage shared by

---

4. See Turner, *Power*, 270. These changes are subject to the assumption that Luke/Peter had access to a version of the LXX which is very close to, if not the same as the text as we have it today.

5. Witherington, *Acts*, 142; Peterson, *Acts*, 141. Codex B and 076 read μετὰ ταῦτα in agreement with LXX and MT, instead of ἐν ταῖς ἐσχάταις ἡμέραις which is the reading of the rest of the MSS. The latter reading is more difficult as it deviates from the LXX and is therefore to be preferred. Bock, *Acts*, 137.

6. Kik, *Eschatology*, 127-35.

7. See Sproul, *The Last Days According to Jesus*, 85-97.

today's church.⁸ Later, we will return to consider the redemptive movement within the NT itself, but at this stage we simply note that the contemporary church inhabits, in principle, the same "last days" as the early church. It is worth noting here, with others, that it would be an overstatement to assert that the "last days" *begin* at Pentecost. It is one in a series of key events ushering in the "last days." It can be seen from the opening of Luke's gospel that the time of fulfillment was being commenced from Jesus' miraculous birth (Luke 1:17, 32–33, 35, 50–55, 67–80; 2:10–11, 25–32, 38–40).⁹ In adding ἐν ταῖς ἐσχάταις ἡμέραις here, Peter is injecting a sharper sense of eschatological urgency to the Pentecost events.¹⁰ Peter also adds λέγει ὁ θεός (says the Lord) to heighten the prophetic drama and make clear the divine origin of the ecstatic events.¹¹ It is worth observing here that such changes in the text demonstrate the "lack of concern . . . for verbal exactness: it is the meaning rather than the words themselves that are important."¹² The adaptations make the quotation fit the context and are characteristic of contemporary exegesis.¹³ It is the emphasis which is important, not the emendation *per se*.

ἐκχεῶ ἀπὸ τοῦ πνεύματός μου ἐπὶ πᾶσαν σάρκα
(I will pour out my Spirit upon all flesh)

---

8. Barrett, *Acts 1–14*, 136.

9. Peterson, *Acts,* 141. See also Menzies who states that although Pentecost "constitutes irrefutable proof that 'the last days' have arrived, it is one in a series of such events [beginning with Jesus' birth and continuing into his entire ministry] and does not mark the beginning of 'the last days.'" *Early Christian Pneumatology*, 216; Turner, *Power,* 352–53.

10. Spencer, *Journeying Through Acts*, 45; Johnson, *The Acts of the Apostles*, 49.

11. MSS A, ℵ, B read ὁ θεός, whereas D, E read κύριος. Metzger favours ὁ θεός based on external evidence and geographical distribution of witnesses. Metzger, *Textual Commentary,* 256–57. Either way the purpose of the addition remains the same.

12. Ellis, "Quotations (in the New Testament)," 995.

13. Alexander, "This is That," 61.

The term ἐκχεῶ (pour out) suggests an "unprecedented deluge of God's Spirit (cf. Isa 32:15; 44:3)."[14] Whatever experience of the Spirit Israel had in the Old Testament, Pentecost was something new and different. In the OT the predominant picture appears to be of the Holy Spirit dwelling among and with the people of God, anointing particular individuals for specific tasks.[15] Now the promise is that all God's people will enjoy the permanent personal presence of God by his Holy Spirit—this special relationship is for the many not just the few. The idea of ἐκχεῶ picks up on Ezekiel's vision of the water flowing from the temple (Ezek 47:1–12). Interestingly the same verb (ἐκχεῶ) appears in the LXX of Ezek 39:29 where God promises to bring his people back from exile and pour his Spirit out upon them. The events witnessed by the watching crowd are evidence of what the prophets foretold—namely the pouring out of the Spirit at the restoration of Israel.[16] The "restoration of Israel" as a theme will be more fully explored in chapter 2, but here we note imagery of pouring out is repeatedly used to signify the transforming personal presence of God with every individual believer.

The verb, ἐκχεῶ, occurs in five other places in Acts. Two refer to the rather gruesome pouring out of Judas' intestines (1:18), and the pouring out of Stephen's blood (22:20). The other three refer to this event (2:17–18, 33) and the parallel event for Gentiles (10:45).[17] Significantly, in 2:33 we learn that it is Jesus, God's resurrected vindicated Messiah, who is responsible for this pouring out. The wider context, when we come to examine it in chapter 2, will illuminate further the meaning of this event.

---

14. Peterson, *Acts*, 141. See also BDAG 3122:b; L&N 59.50.

15. For example Exod 31:3; Num 11:26; Jdgs 3:10; 1 Sam 10:10. See Hamilton, *God's Indwelling Presence*, 25–56.

16. Cf. Isa 32:15; 44:3; Ezek 36:26–7; 37:14.

17. Chapter 3 will examine whether it is correct to consider Acts 10:45–46 the Gentile Pentecost.

Ἀπο (from) plus the genitive, τοῦ πνεύματός (the Spirit) is probably partitive here.[18] The partitive use is governed by the verb, rather than making any theological statement about partial or subsequent Spirit-fillings.[19] The precise meaning of the phrase πᾶσαν σάρκα (all flesh), with the qualification surrounding "*your* sons and daughters" and "*my* slaves", will need "fleshing out" below. As will be seen the promise is for Israel first.[20] Importantly, the universal note of the expression means all without distinction rather than all without exception. Whereas, in the Old Testament the Spirit was given to kings, leaders, prophets and other special individuals, now the Spirit will be for all God's servants. Through the development of the narrative, Luke shows, and Peter comes to realise, how Samaritans and Gentiles come to share in the promise.[21] The LXX and the majority of MSS read πᾶσαν σάρκα. Codex D has πάσας σάρκας, changing the singular to the plural. This may reflect a universalistic perspective in D and therefore the majority reading should be followed.[22]

καὶ προφητεύσουσιν οἱ υἱοὶ ὑμῶν καὶ αἱ θυγατέρες ὑμῶν
(And your sons and your daughters shall prophesy)

Prophecy is here shown to be the necessary and deliberate result of God pouring out his Spirit—it was to enable all God's people to prophesy—it is the fulfillment of Moses' desire in Numbers 11:29. The precise nature of this prophecy is debated and further exploration will be undertaken in chapter 3. At this point it is worth briefly considering some common explanations. Calvin thought

---

18. BDAG 105:a; Bruce, *Acts*, 121; Bock, *Acts*, 113 *contra* Barrett, *Acts 1–14*, 136. Culy and Parsons also suggest it could be a genitive of source. Culy and Parsons, *Acts*, 34.

19. Culy and Parsons, *Acts*, 34. This addresses Barrett's difficulty in Barrett, *Acts 1–14*, 136.

20. Johnson, *Acts*, 49. See also Acts 3:26.

21. Peterson, *Acts*, 140–41; Bock, *Acts*, 113.

22. Rius-Camps and Read-Heimerdinger, *The Message of Acts in Codex Bezae* 1:182; Bock, *Proclamation*, 158.

An Exegesis of Acts 2:17–21

it meant that "all men shall be endued with spiritual wisdom, even to the prophetical excellency."[23] He appeals to Jer 31:34, but that text does not mention prophecy explicitly.[24] Similarly Stott, following Luther, proposes it is the universal knowledge of God through Christ by the Spirit.[25] This is surely part of the answer, but does not account for the diverse range of prophetic activity seen within Acts. Many Acts scholars have noted that the Spirit in the Old Testament was the Spirit of prophecy, and suggest that is what is poured out here,[26] and part of the answer must relate to the already observed phenomenon of tongues-speech.[27] Prophecy is part of the explanation for the ecstatic declarative utterances.

The verb itself, προφητεύσουσιν (they will prophesy), is rare in Acts occurring only here, 19:6 (also connected with tongues-speech), and 21:9 (Philip's daughters). The related noun (προφήτης—prophet) is more common, occurring fifty-nine times in Luke-Acts (thirty times in Acts), although the overwhelming majority of those examples refer to OT prophets.[28] Examples of NT prophets occur in Acts 11:27; 13:1; 15:32; 21:10. Aune proposes that prophecy in Acts includes prediction (11:27–28); appointing individuals to tasks (13:1–3); solving disputes (15:28, 32); and guidance (16:6–10).[29] It is worth remembering that there was variety in prophetic ministry within the OT. Some are evidently "professional prophets" (Amos 7:14),[30] some are preachers and teachers (Mal

23. Calvin, *Acts*, 87.
24. Ibid.
25. Stott, *The Message of Acts*, 74.
26. For example Dunn, "Baptism in the Spirit," 8; Schweizer, "πνεῦμα," 407–409; Turner, "The Spirit of Prophecy," 333–34; Menzies, *Development*, 224–25.
27. Fitzmyer, *Acts*, 253; Bock, *Acts*, 113.
28. Dunn, *Acts*, 29.
29. Aune, *Prophecy in Early Christianity*, 192.
30. This may have been as court or cultic prophets. Court prophets apparently included men like Nathan and Gad (2 Sam 24:11; 2 Chr 29:25). Cultic or temple prophets are seen in 1 Sam 10:5. Lindblom suggests that there

4:4),³¹ some are leaders of music and singing (1 Chr 25:1–8; 2 Chr 30:14–23),³² and others proclaim messages received from God (1 Kings 22:14). On numerous occasions people engage in prophetic activity without bearing the official title of "prophet" (Num 11:25; 1 Sam 10:6; 19:23).³³ The diachronic development within the OT suggests that the earlier more ecstatic prophets gradually give way to those who have more formal roles proclaiming God's words or organizing and leading cultic worship. Nevertheless, a measure of diversity remains cautioning against too narrowly defining the OT prophet. In chapter 3, we shall see that the diversity is carried into the NT, but for now the pouring out of the Spirit on all flesh means that all are, to some degree, prophets.³⁴ Menzies suggests that Luke's usage of "prophet/prophecy" is flexible such that every member of the community could possess the Spirit of prophecy, yet there could still be some who exercise a special "prophetic" ministry.³⁵ Similarly, Schweizer proposes evidence of both dynamic and animistic functions of the Holy Spirit in Acts.³⁶ Dynamic function indicates a general endowment of the Spirit on all Christians (Acts 2:38; 5:32; 6:3; 10:45; 11:24). Animistic function indicates a special endowment of the Spirit on particular individuals for specific tasks (Acts 4:8, 31; 7:55; 13:9).³⁷

---

may have been a degree of overlap in these roles and also notes that while some prophets were part of guilds, others seem much freer. See Lindblom, *Prophecy in Ancient Israel*, 75–83.

31. HALOT 2:661–62.

32. Lindblom, *Prophecy in Ancient Israel*, 218.

33. Verhoef, "Prophecy" in *NIDOTTE* 4:1070. Also David is identified as a prophet in Acts 2:30, without having been referred to as one in the OT.

34. An idea we will return to later is that prophets and prophecy are not all of the same type and degree. The considerable semantic range in the use of the vocabulary means it is not necessary to consider all prophets or prophecy on a par with the likes of Isaiah, Jeremiah or Ezekiel.

35. Menzies, *Development*, 228.

36. Schweizer, "πνεῦμα," 406.

37. Schweizer explains this in less technical terms in Schweizer, *The Holy Spirit*, 75–76. This distinction is also noted by Ferguson, *The Holy Spirit*, 89;

An Exegesis of Acts 2:17-21

καὶ οἱ νεανίσκοι ὑμῶν ὁράσεις ὄψονται καὶ οἱ πρεσβύτεροι ὑμῶν ἐνυπνίοις ἐνυπνιασθήσονται·

(And your young men will see visions, and your old men will dream dreams)

The "visions" and "dreams" mentioned are probably not meant to be taken apart from the "prophecy" previously mentioned since such activities were part of the prophetic ministry in the Old Testament.[38] Further, the visions and dreams here sit in synonymous parallelism, rather than being two radically distinct activities."[39] Visions will go on to play an important role for Luke within the unfolding narrative directing and guiding missionary endeavour.[40] The dative ἐνυπνίοις (dreams) followed by its cognate verb reflects the Hebrew infinitive absolute construction which intensifies the verbal idea.[41] Since God is at work the blessings of his Spirit are sure and certain. The two age groups mentioned here (in conjunction with the sons and daughters in the previous clause) again emphasizes the universal scope of Spirit's reception, and Spirit-inspired ministry. The whole community had "prophetic" gifts. The order of "young" and "old" is reversed from

---

Hamilton, *God's Indwelling Presence*, 183-203. I do not follow Hamilton in seeing a strict separation in meaning between πλήρης/πληρόω and πίμπλημι. He argues that πλήρης/πληρόω is used in Schweizer's 'dynamic' sense, and that πίμπλημι is used in Schweizer's 'animistic' sense. I think this is generally helpful, but I see a degree of semantic overlap in these terms (see for example 2:4; 7:55; 9:17; 13:52—these are examples where I think strict semantic distinction is open to question).

38. 1 Sam 3:15; 2 Sam 7:17; Isa 1:1; Jer 23:28; Ezek 1:1; Oba 1:1; Nah 1:1. Peterson, *Acts*, 141.

39. Barrett, *Acts 1-14*, 137, *contra* Fitzmyer who states "The Spirit will affect young and old alike, but in different ways." Fitzmyer, *Acts*, 253.

40. Acts 7:31, 55-56; 9:3-10; 10:3, 17, 19; 11:5; 16:9-10; 18:9; 27:23. Johnson, *Acts*, 49.

41. Wallace, *Greek Grammar Beyond the Basics*, 168-69. BDF §198 suggests a dative of association, but that is based on a grammatical possibility within the Greek text rather than reflecting the intention of the Hebrew construction.

9

LXX and MT perhaps because those who first received the gift on Pentecost were themselves young.[42] The qualification of the nouns with ὑμῶν (your) suggests that the prophecy was addressed first to Israel.[43] As Luke's narrative unfolds it is clear that the promise is for *all* who will call on the name of the Lord regardless of ethnicity, but at this stage the promise is announced first to Israel. This will be important in considering the function of the prophetic fulfillment in its wider literary context.

Verse 18

καὶ γε ἐπὶ τοὺς δούλους μου καὶ ἐπὶ τὰς δούλας μου ἐν ταῖς ἡμέραις ἐκείναις ἐκχεῶ ἀπὸ τοῦ πνεύματός μού καὶ προφητεύσουσιν

(And even upon my male servants and my female servants, in those days, I will pour out my Spirit, and they shall prophesy)

The emphatic particle γε, best rendered "even", stresses that this gift is even for the lowest classes of servant, both male and female.[44] The pronoun μου (my), which follows δούλους (male servants) and δούλας (female servants), is absent in D, LXX and MT, and is another addition to the Joel text.[45] The addition clarifies that the promise concerns specifically those who are truly God's servants, rather than all without exception.[46] The "pouring out" and prophecy are again linked, and, as with previous clauses, the stress is on the promise being for all classes of people. Acts 2:17–18

---

42. Bruce, *Acts*, 121.

43. The majority of MSS and the LXX have four occurences of ὑμῶν in the verse. Codex D has two occurences of αὐτῶν and omits two. As has already been mentioned, this perhaps reflects a universalist tendency in D.

44. BDF §439; Bock, *Acts*, 114.

45. D also omits ἐν ταῖς ἡμέραις ἐκείναις. LXX, MT and the majority of MSS include the phrase.

46. Johnson, *Acts*, 49. Peterson, *Acts*, 140.

signifies a barrier-breaking event; people of all classes, genders and ages will receive, and partake of, the promise. This is contrary to the Pentecostal doctrine of subsequence which appears to create further barriers between categories of believers.[47]

The second mention of prophesying is an addition to the LXX and MT of the Joel quotation, perhaps for emphasis, and perhaps to form an *inclusio* with v. 17c.[48] If Luke added these words they perhaps demonstrate the high value he places upon prophecy.[49] So far the application of Joel 3:1–5 to the events of Pentecost emphasizes the universality of the promise (male and female, young and old, slave and (tacitly) free) and the Spirit's presence with all believers for revelatory and proclamatory functions. How we understand these functions will be enlarged upon as our investigation proceeds.

Verse 19–20

καὶ δώσω τέρατα ἐν τῷ οὐρανῷ ἄνω καὶ σημεῖα ἐπὶ τῆς γῆς κάτω
(And I will give wonders in the heaven above and signs upon the earth below)

Joel 3:3 (LXX) has only καὶ δώσω τέρατα ἐν τῷ οὐρανῷ καὶ ἐπὶ τῆς γῆς (and I will give wonders in the heaven and upon the earth). Acts 2:19 adds ἄνω (above), καὶ σημεῖα (and signs) and κάτω (below). Richard Pervo plausibly suggests the addition of the prepositions may be to "provide each of the clauses with an end rhyme."[50] The addition of σημεῖα (signs) deliberately evokes all the theological import of the OT phrase "signs and wonders". Signs and wonders are frequently paired in Acts and in the Old

---

47. Zwiep, "Luke's Understanding of Baptism in the Holy Spirit," 138–39.
48. D also omits the word probably to follow LXX and MT. Turner, *Power*, 270.
49. Menzies, *Development*, 221; Barrett, *Acts*, 137.
50. Pervo, *Acts*, 79. So too Bock, *Acts*, 115; Bruce, *Acts*, 121.

Testament.[51] In the OT, the phrase "signs and wonders" is almost universally associated with the events of the exodus, when God redeemed his people from slavery. Of the fifteen occurrences of σημεῖα with τέρατα in the OT, ten refer to the events of the exodus (Exod 11:9, 10; Deut 6:22; 7:19; 11:3; 28:46; 29:2; Ps 77:43; 134:9; Jer 39:20), two refer to Isaiah's ministry (Isa 8:18; 20:3), and three are found in the book of Daniel (4:1, 2: 6:28). Marshall also notes that the theophanic language is particularly associated with Sinai.[52] The exact nature of what is being referred to here requires us to examine the next phrase. What seems clear is that signs and wonders are tied to God's redemptive activity—"This is the time of new deliverance to which God bears witness."[53] When they are present it is certain that God is doing something that is redemptively hugely significant. Johnson also suggests that Luke has "made the text foretell the working of 'wonders and signs', which he uses to identify the prophetic figures in his story."[54] Where signs and wonders are found, so are God's authoritative, to-be-obeyed, spokesmen.

> αἷμα καὶ πῦρ καὶ ἀτμίδα καπνοῦ. ὁ ἥλιος μεταστραφήσεται εἰς σκότος καὶ ἡ σελήνη εἰς αἷμά πρὶν ἐλθεῖν ἡμέραν κυρίου τὴν μεγάλην καὶ ἐπιφανῆ[55]
>
> (blood and fire and clouds of smoke. The sun will be changed into darkness and the moon into blood before the great and awesome day of the Lord comes)

---

51. Parsons, *Acts,* 43. Acts 2:22, 43; 4:30; 5:12; 6:8; 7:36; 14:3; 15:12; and in the OT: Exod 7:3; Deut 4:34; 6:22; 26:8; 29:3; 34:11; Neh 9:10; Ps 135:9; Dan 6:27.

52. Marshall, "Acts," 535.

53. Bock, *Acts,* 115.

54. Johnson, *Acts,* 49.

55. Codex D omits αἷμα καὶ πῦρ καὶ ἀτμίδα καπνοῦ perhaps because of error, or perhaps because of perceived lack of fulfilment. MT, LXX and the majority of MSS include the phrase so it should be retained. Bock, *Proclamation,* 159.

An Exegesis of Acts 2:17-21

Here we move into the realm of things that appear even less straightforward. First, a literal darkened sun and blood red moon are initially perturbing cosmic spectacles, but we must remember that Bible writers employ such terms idiomatically.[56] Second, although Johnson thinks there is a distinction to be made between the "signs and wonders" carried out by the apostles, and the cosmic portents which usher in final judgment,[57] syntactically such a decision is difficult to justify. The first part of this phrase is epexegetical, further explaining what God's redemptive signs and wonders will look like, using language reminiscent of the Egyptian plagues.[58] Given the epexegetical nature of the phrase, we need to examine more closely the referent of the "wonders and signs". Scholarly opinion has included: i) the miracles of Jesus; ii) the cosmic signs accompanying the crucifixion; iii) the Pentecost phenomena; iv) the miracles of the disciples; v) the cosmic portents accompanying the "day of the Lord" (which could be the final *parousia*, AD 70, or, more generally, world-shaking historical events).[59] We will examine each in turn before drawing conclusions on likely meanings.

THE MIRACLES OF JESUS

This is clearly the referent in 2:22 where the more unusual order of wonders then signs is preserved. This would make sense of the addition of "signs" to the verse.[60] Whether the description in 2:17 primarily refers to Jesus' earthly ministry is debatable. The καὶ (and) at the start of v. 19 connects it closely with what prece-

---

56. See for example Isa 13:10; 34:4; Ezek 32:7.
57. Johnson, *Acts*, 50.
58. Culy and Parsons describe it as an appositional phrase. Culy and Parsons, *Acts*, 35.
59. Menzies, *Development*, 222.
60. Sloan, "Signs and Wonders: A Rhetorical Clue to the Pentecost Discourse," 235–37. Likewise, Woodhouse, "Signs and Wonders and Evangelical Ministry," 21.

ded which clearly referred to "all flesh".[61] Further, we see apostles performing signs and wonders in the ensuing narrative (e.g. 2:43; 5:12), and, if Johnson is right that "signs and wonders" authenticate key characters, it would seem strange that the exclusive referent here is to Christ and his ministry. It may be part of the answer but is not the whole.

The cosmic signs accompanying the crucifixion

Bruce and Larkin see here a reference to Jesus' death.[62] Bruce notes that at the crucifixion the crowd had seen a darkened sun, and later that same day may also have seen a blood-red full moon.[63] Such events were clearly harbingers of the great and glorious day of the Lord. However, as Bock notes, αἷμα (blood) appears 19 times in Acts and none of the uses allude to the description of Jesus' death in Luke 23.[64] More problematic is that the fire and smoke mentioned in Acts 2:19 are not accounted for in this view. For this reason, and those cited under i), while there may be some allusion back to Christ's death, it would be difficult to conclude that this was the only or even primary referent.

The phenomena accompanying Pentecost

Fitzmyer thinks Luke is using apocalyptic language to describe what those in Jerusalem had just seen in the Pentecost event. The description reflects the noise and fire just experienced.[65] Whilst the previous view failed to account for the language of fire and smoke, this view fails to account for the language of darkened sun and blood-red moon.

---

61. Acts 2:17.
62. Bruce, *Acts*, 61–62; Larkin, *Acts*, 53.
63. Bruce, *Acts*, 62.
64. Bock, *Acts*, 115.
65. Fitzmyer, *Acts*, 253.

Montague sees significance in the reversal of the order of terms, from the more common "signs and wonders" to the more unusual "wonders and signs."[66] The significance, for Montague, is in noting the one place in the LXX where the order is also reversed (Wis 10:16–11:1) where reference is made to the Lord's servant making the tongues of those who could not speak eloquent. It is a stimulating proposal but relies heavily on the thesis that the reversal of order is a *deliberate* allusion to Wis 10:16–11:1. Such a thesis is speculative and difficult to prove. O'Reilly is more persuasive in arguing that the word order is of little significance.[67]

THE MIRACLES OF THE APOSTLES

Miracles performed by apostles appear in 2:43 immediately after the speech and in the same order (wonders then signs) as in 2:19. The strategic placement of the phrase in 2:43 and its significance through the rest of the book means this view has much in its favour.[68] Further, this is not at odds with view i) since the signs and wonders are not from the disciples alone, but from the Spirit's empowerment poured out by Christ from heaven.[69] In that sense they also are part of what Jesus is *continuing* to do in his exaltation (Acts 1:1).

THE COSMIC PORTENTS ACCOMPANYING THE "DAY OF THE LORD"

This is the majority view, but is complicated by the fact that it encompasses a range of subset views. First, many take this to be a reference to God's final judgment, qualified by the phrase "the great and glorious day of the Lord," which is elsewhere in the NT called "the day of the Lord Jesus" (2 Cor 1:14), or the "day of Christ" (Phil

---

66. Montague, *Holy Spirit: Growth of a Biblical Tradition*, 285–86.
67. O'Reilly, *Word and Sign*, 165 n8.
68. Sloan, "Signs and Wonders," 235.
69. See also 4:30 where the believers pray to the Lord to stretch out his hand to perform signs and wonders.

1:10).⁷⁰ Conzelmann says the transition in Acts 2:19 from present to future comports with Luke 21:7–36.⁷¹

Second, Marshall considers τέρατα to refer to cosmic portents of final judgment, while σημεῖα alludes to miracles in Acts.⁷² This view, while accounting for ἄνω and κάτω, fails to take into account the numerous times when both signs *and* wonders are attributed to the apostles in Acts.⁷³ It is too neat a distinction between the two.

Third, Calvin understands the language to speak of figurative tokens of God's wrath "through the whole frame of the world."⁷⁴ Stott, similarly, suggests that the reference is to "convulsions of history (since this is traditional apocalyptic imagery for times of social and political revolution)."⁷⁵

The fourth option sees the language to be in line with passages such as Luke 21, Matt 24 and Mark 13, with the primary referent being the destruction of Jerusalem in AD 70. Close conceptual connections between Joel's prophecy and those of Isa 13:10 and Ezek 32:7 would suggest that what is spoken of here is the physical judgment upon the nation which rejects and rebels against God—in this case Jerusalem.⁷⁶ Further, the wider context of Joel speaks of the invasion and destruction of Zion.⁷⁷ What is notable is that the cosmic signs do not accompany, but rather *precede* the "great day" with πρὶν pointing to subsequent time.⁷⁸ The problem with this view is that "signs and wonders" are attributed to the apostles and others numerous times in Acts as narrative fulfillment of Peter's

---

70. Bock, *Acts*, 116–17; Peterson, *Acts*, 143; Polhill, *Acts*, 110; Witherington, *Acts*, 143.

71. Conzelmann, *Acts*, 20.

72. Marshall, *Acts*, 74.

73. Acts 2:43; 4:30; 5:12; 6:8; 14:3; 15:12.

74. Calvin, *Acts*, 89.

75. Stott, *Acts*, 75. Isa 13:9–13; Ezek 32:7–8; Amos 8:9; Matt 24:29.

76. Jordan, *Through New Eyes*, 64–66.

77. Ibid. See also Kik, *An Eschatology of Victory*, 129–33.

78. BDF §383; 395; Bock, *Acts*, 117; Wallace, *Greek Grammar*, 596.

pesher sermon. Further, as has already been mentioned, for this view to work, the "last days" and the "glorious day of the Lord" would have to be defined as that period of time running up to and culminating in the events of AD 70. This view is possible but, given 2 Pet 3:1–13, it is unlikely that AD 70 is the sole or even primary referent.

To conclude, a combination of these views is best.[79] This may seem like a spectacularly acute case of fence-sitting. However, in view of the eschatological telescoping employed by the insertion of ἐν ταῖς ἐσχάταις ἡμέραις in v. 17 we could view the "signs and wonders" as referring to a series of events including Jesus' miracles, his death, Pentecost, apostolic miracles, AD 70, historical events and final *parousia*, as all testifying to the in-breaking and presence of the new eschatological age. It may even embrace the miraculous events of Jesus' birth as well.[80] These "cosmic" events all demonstrate that the King is enthroned and his Kingdom rule has begun.

There is probably a textual error in the LXX regarding the word ἐπιφανῆ. It appears they read נוֹרָא as being a niphal participle from the root ראה (see) rather than ירא (awesome).[81] The referent of this "day of the Lord" is most naturally the day of final deliverance and judgment, as elsewhere in the NT.[82]

Verse 21

καὶ ἔσται πᾶς ὃς ἂν ἐπικαλέσηται τὸ ὄνομα κυρίου σωθήσεται

(And it will be that all who will call upon the name of the Lord will be saved)

---

79. Peterson, *Acts*, 143.

80. Menzies, *Development*, 223.

81. Conzelmann, *Acts*, 20. MSS D and a omit καὶ ἐπιφανῆ perhaps for this reason. The same error can be seen in the LXX of Mal 3:23.

82. See 1 Cor 1:8; 5:5; 2 Cor 1:14; Phil 1:10; 2:16; 2 Tim 1:18.

The necessity of calling upon the name of the Lord is evident given the presence of the last days and the immanence of the glorious day. These climactic words pave the way for the proclamation of Christ which follows, with its subsequent invitation to repentance, faith and baptism.[83] Although the "all" will later come to include Gentiles, at this stage the promise explicitly concerns every Israelite.[84] The "name of the Lord" will play an important role in the narrative as we come to see that his name is Jesus (Acts 4:10, 12).[85] His name is now the only way to salvation and is invoked in healing (3:6). If an allusion to the wider context of Joel is meant, by way of metalepsis, the salvation spoken of involves future deliverance from judgement and the restoration of Israel (Joel 3:5—4:1 LXX).

Salvation is a central motif for Luke, as Dunn observes: "The story of Jesus and about the Spirit is the story of salvation or it amounts to nothing."[86] Salvation for Luke is holistic—it includes the social, physical and spiritual dimension.[87] As Wright says, Jesus saves "wholes not souls."[88] This holistic salvation is a hallmark of Lucan soteriology, and is indicative of the in-breaking of the Kingdom of God.[89] It is also noteworthy within the context of this discussion to observe that the giving of the Spirit is a necessity if people are going to "call upon the name of the Lord" and is

---

83. Fitzmyer, *Acts,* 254.

84. Gaventa, *Acts,* 77; *Pace* Fitzmyer, *Acts,* 254.

85. Read-Heimerdinger, *The Bezan Text of Acts,* 279. Commenting on 2:36, Kavin Rowe helpfully points out that the statement, "God has made this Jesus, whom you crucified, both Lord and Christ" is epistemological rather than ontological *contra* adoptionist Christologies. Rowe, *Early Narrative Christology,* 194.

86. Dunn, *Acts,* 29.

87. Witherington, *Acts,* 143.

88. Wright, *Surprised by Hope,* 211.

89. Witherington, "Salvation and Health in Christian Antiquity," 164–66; Marshall, *Luke: Historian and Theologian,* 95–96; Bock, *Luke 1:1–9:50,* 33–34.

An Exegesis of Acts 2:17-21

therefore essential for salvation.[90] It is not merely a *donum superadditum* for empowering witness.[91]

Finally, it is also worth noting that Peter omits the final words of Joel 3:5 which refer to the deliverance for Mount Zion and Jerusalem. Perhaps the omission comports with the thesis that part of the fulfilment of the judgment spoken of in vv. 18–19 refers to events in Jerusalem around AD 70. The omission may also be due to Peter's reticence to particularise Jerusalem as sole referent of the promise.[92]

SUMMARY AND CONCLUSION

This chapter has sought to examine Acts 2:17–21 in terms of the meaning and relationships of words and phrases, as well as the significance of changes to the LXX and MT of Joel 3:1–5. Pertinent observations from this exegesis are as follows.

First, the addition of the term ἐν ταῖς ἐσχάταις ἡμέραις brings the age of the NT church into "the last days". Given that we are still in the period of the last days it seems reasonable to conclude that the promise, however we understand it, still in some way stands. God will continue to pour out his Spirit upon his servants, accompanied by prophetic activity and signs and wonders, and those who call on the name of the Lord will be saved. Whether the understanding of some elements of the promise needs refining remains to be seen but what is important at this stage is to affirm that the church inhabits the same "last days" of which Peter spoke.

Second, and also related to one significant addition to the Joel text, prophecy is important for Luke. Twice we are told that believers will prophesy (2:17, 18), and prophetic speech will play an important part in the narrative. It remains to be seen exactly what the term refers too, but it will not do at this stage to sweep prophecy

---

90. Witherington, *Acts*, 140.
91. Turner, "Spirit of Prophecy," 347 *contra* Menzies, *Development*, 48.
92. Sleeman, *Geography and the Ascension Narrative*, 99.

under the carpet as unimportant for the life of the church in the last days. All who call on the name of the Lord have the "Spirit of prophecy."

Third, the promise is for all. The pairings of sons and daughters, young and old, and male and female servants stress that the promise is for all of God's people without distinction. All will be indwelt and empowered by the Spirit to be his spokespersons.

Fourth, and little considered to thus far, the meaning of the quotation is primarily Christological. The pouring out of the Spirit confirms what Jesus promised in Acts 1:5. It attests to God's exaltation of him as Messiah. When we consider the wider speech, Peter's purpose in citing Joel 3:1–5 (LXX) is not primarily as an *apologia* for the Pentecost miracle events in and of themselves, but as evidence of the Lordship of Christ. Luke's primary use of the OT is "proclamatory not apologetic."[93] This leads us to more fully consider the surrounding context of Acts 2:17–21, namely Acts 1–2. How does the prophetic motif of restoration fit in with Luke's introduction to his second volume?

---

93. Bock, *Proclamation*, 167.

2

Acts 2:17–21 Within the Context of Acts 1–2

INTRODUCTION

HAVING UNDERTAKEN an initial examination of the verses in relation to one another, we now move to consider how the immediate literary context contributes to an understanding of Acts 2:17–21. To address rightly the place of Acts 2:17–21 within the wider charismatic debate, we must understand its function in its surrounding context—narrowly, Acts 1–2, and more broadly, the rest of Acts. In chapter 3 we will consider Acts 2:17–21 in relation to the rest of Acts, but here we will consider these verses in the context of Acts 1–2. These opening two chapters function as Luke's introduction to his second volume—Walton likens them to an overture, with all the main themes present, to the rest of the book.[1] We will first consider Jesus' promise and ascension in Acts 1. Then we will move to consider the events of Pentecost in 2:1–13. Finally, we shall consider the speech of 2:14–39. All of this will lead to a richer understanding of the purpose and meaning of Acts 2:17–21.

It is worth saying at the outset that my hermeneutical approach to these chapters is a maximalist one in regard to intertextualities—that is to say I am sympathetic to the possibility of

1. Walton argues this persuasively, having conducted a thorough linguistic analysis. Walton, "Where Does the Beginning of Acts End?" 467.

allusions to other passages and themes within the OT. The reasons for this are as follows. First, Luke himself encourages the search for the fulfilment of OT themes in Luke 24:27. There Jesus tells the disciples that the OT Scriptures point to and are fulfilled in him. When we recall that Luke's second volume is about what the risen Jesus continues to do and teach (Acts 1:1) we are permitted to look for fulfilments of OT promises, themes or ideas. Second, Luke has a careful and deliberate narrative style which requires the reader to entertain intertextual possibilities more seriously (Luke 1:1–4). Pervo identifies evidence of Luke's narrative care in identifying a number of narrative devices such as pace, repetition, parallels, duplication, interlacement, cycles, mimesis and symbolism.[2] Maxwell has also identified a number of rhetorical strategies employed by Luke to stimulate audience participation, filling gaps and joining dots.[3] Third, Luke's Greek is what Loveday Alexander has called "biblical Greek", indicative of a writer soaked in the biblical sources, and having had a Jewish education. Again, this means linguistic echoes ought not to be dismissed as mere coincidences.[4] The allusions and echoes are Luke's way of conveying the theological significance of the events he describes.

PROMISE, ASCENSION AND RECONSTITUTION: ACTS 1:1–26

This chapter will argue that the restoration of Israel and the new exodus are prominent themes in the opening chapters of Acts. The end of Luke's first volume has seen the lamb slaughtered, the tyrant mortally wounded, and redemption accomplished. What becomes now of this new Israel? They are being prepared to be a light to the nations.[5]

2. Pervo, *The Mystery of Acts*, 55–90.

3. Maxwell, *Hearing Between the Lines*, 119–75.

4. Alexander, "Septuaginta, Fachprosa, Imitatio," 246; See also Payne, "Semitisms in the Book of Acts," 134–50; Padilla, "Hellenistic παιδεια and Luke's Education," 436–37.

5. Peterson, *Acts*, 112; Wall, *Acts*, 42.

Acts 2:17-21 Within the Context of Acts 1-2

There are a number of conceptual and Scriptural allusions, as well as more explicit references, which back up this thesis. As Turner notes, "Acts 1:3-8 is ... one of the most subtle and concentrated pieces of theological writing in Luke's whole enterprise."[6] We will note here eight Scriptural allusions:

First, there is the forty day teaching and preparation period the disciples spend with the resurrected Jesus (1:3)—a number rich in symbolism for Israel.[7] Moses spent forty years in preparation for his mission; for forty years Israel wandered in the wilderness before taking the land (Ex 16:35); and for forty days Moses was on the Mount Sinai receiving the Ten Commandments (Ex 24:18). Forty days is also the number of days Jesus was tested before his own public Spirit-anointed ministry began (Luke 4:2, 18-19). The number forty is redemptively significant, and symbolic of a waiting or preparation period before the work begins.[8]

Second, they are told to wait in Jerusalem (Acts 1:4)—a city rich in historical and theological significance.[9] Jerusalem was the place where God ruled over and blessed his people through his king,[10] and the place where nations would stream to hear the word of the Lord.[11] In Acts, there is a distinction to be made between the symbolic and topographic cartography of Jerusalem. Luke portrays Jerusalem both positively and negatively. Positively, Jerusalem is a centre of restoration and Messianic hope (Luke 2:38). Luke's gospel begins and ends in Jerusalem (Luke 2:22; 24:52), with Jerusalem both

---

6. Turner, *Power*, 294-95.
7. Spencer, *Acts*, 35; Pervo, *Acts*, 37; *Contra* Bock, *Acts*, 55.
8. Robinson and Wall, *Called to be Church*, 32; Talbert, *Reading Acts*, 23-24; Balz, "τεσσεράκοντα," 136.
9. Fitzmyer, *Acts*, 204.
10. 2 Sam 7; 1 Kgs 8; Ps 78; Green, *The Word of His Grace*, 43.
11. Isa 2:2-4; 40:1-2; 65:18-25; Zech 8:20-23; Mic 4:1-8. Peterson, *Acts*, 107; Spencer, *Acts*, 36.

the destination city, and the resurrection city for Jesus (Luke 9:51; 24:1–8). In Acts, Jerusalem is the launch city of mission (Acts 1:8), and each new wave of expansion circles back to Jerusalem.[12] Negatively, Jerusalem is the city which kills prophets, and the city in which the Messiah is killed (Luke 13:33–34), and as such the city will be judged accordingly (Luke 21:24).[13] There is also the ominous final closing of the temple doors (Acts 21:30).[14] Jerusalem is simultaneously a symbol of restoration, a centre of salvation, and a place of judgement.[15] While the Jewish leadership will be judged for killing the Messiah, Jerusalem, as a symbol of restoration, as we have it in Acts 1:4, 8, still stands.[16]

Third, there is the unusual mention of the ἐπαγγελίαν τοῦ πατρὸς (the promise of the Father (1:4); cf. Luke 24:49). Why is Luke using this phrase, and to what is he alluding? Options abound here with four in particular vying for attention. First, it could be a reference back to Luke 11:13, where Jesus affirms that the Holy Spirit is the gift of the Father. Second, Menzies considers the Joel quotation in 2:17–21 to be the most obvious candidate, as that is the Scripture appealed to in demonstrating that the promise of the Father is now received (Acts 2:33).[17] Third, Dunn argues that the promise

---

12. Acts 12:25; 15:2; 18:22; 19:21; 21:17. Johnson, *Luke*, 15.

13. Weatherly points out that it is more specifically the leaders in Jerusalem who are responsible for the death of Jesus. Weatherly, *Jewish Responsibility for the Death of Jesus in Luke-Acts*, 54–90.

14. Tyson, *Images of Judaism in Luke-Acts*, 184.

15. Fitzmyer, *Luke I-IX*, 168.

16. See also Parsons, "The Place of Jerusalem on the Lukan Landscape," 155–71. Read-Heimerdinger notes the various spellings of Jerusalem (Ἱεροσόλυμα/Ἱερουσαλήμ) in the MSS, and suggests that, with respect to the Alexandrian texts, the different spellings are used to distinguish between "the religious and geographical aspects of the city." Read-Heimerdinger, *The Bezan Text*, 344.

17. Menzies, *Development*, 203.

Acts 2:17-21 Within the Context of Acts 1-2

refers back to well-known new covenant promise passages such as Ezekiel 36 and Jeremiah 31,[18] and although neither text is explicitly referred to, allusions to Sinai in Acts 1-2, coupled with the writing of the law on hearts by the Spirit at Pentecost, strengthen Dunn's case. Fourth, Bock notes the linguistic connections between Isa 32:15 (the Spirit poured out from on high) and Luke 24:49 (being clothed with power from on high).[19] Taking all these things into account, it would seem that the promise spoken about is the Holy Spirit, promised in Luke 11:13 and 12:12, alluded to in Luke 24:49 (likely itself alluding to Isa 32:15), and fulfilled on the day of Pentecost in the pouring out of the Holy Spirit.[20]

Fourth, we hear mention again of John the Baptist (1:5), the figure who fills with expectation (Luke 1:17; 3:15), and announces the coming day of the Lord (Luke 3:16-17; Mal 4:5-6). He is an important figure in the climax of Israel's story as the forerunner of the one who would truly cleanse Israel.[21]

Fifth, there is a more explicit reference in the question of v. 6. It is a natural question given the Lucan connection between the pouring out of the Spirit and the coming of the Kingdom (1:3-5), and also in view of the allusion to the Baptist's prophecy in Luke 3:16-17 with its eschatological overtones.[22] There

18. Dunn, *Baptism in the Holy Spirit*, 47-48.

19. Bock, *Acts*, 56.

20. Pelikan, *Acts*, 41; Lee, "An Evangelical Dialogue on Luke, Salvation and Spirit Baptism," 86.

21. Peterson, *Acts*, 107-08. It is interesting to note how frequently the Baptist is mentioned in Acts—1:5, 22; 10:37; 11:16; 13:24-25; 18:25; 19:4. This could possibly be because the "Baptist movement" continued into the fourth century and was an issue in Luke's day. In that case, part of the reason for his frequent appearances is to demonstrate the need for conversion to Christ (Witherington, *Acts*, 569).

22. Peterson, *Acts*, 108; Fitzmyer, *Acts*, 205; Bock, *Acts*, 62; *contra* Calvin who writes, "There are as many errors in this question as words." Calvin, *Acts*, 43. Pervo also, wrongly in my view, describes the question as "excruciatingly inept", Pervo, *Acts*, 41.

is also a connection in early Judaism between the appointed time and restoration.²³ The question is included as a literary device, anticipating misconception and inviting further clarification.²⁴ The interpreter must decide whether the ἀλλὰ (but) at the start of v. 8 is sharply contrastive or perhaps more continuative. I am inclined to think the second alternative more accurately represents what is happening, particularly given the Isaiah allusions in v. 8 to which we shortly turn, and the positive mention of restoration made by Peter in Acts 3:20–21.²⁵ Jesus' answer suggests that kingdom restoration is on the agenda but in a much broader and all-encompassing fashion than was expected.²⁶ It is also worth noting that Jesus is the agent of this restoration,²⁷ as much of what follows, as was mentioned in the previous chapter, is Christological.²⁸

Sixth, we also see scriptural allusions in 1:8. When taken together with Luke 24:49, these verses speak of the Spirit coming upon the disciples from on high which may be an allusion to Isa 32:15, a verse appearing in a context which speaks of the restoration of Israel.²⁹ Similarly the mention of witnesses picks up Isa 43:10–12, and witnessing "to the ends of the earth" alludes to Isa 49:6 (which is also cited by Paul in Acts 13:47) which is also a chapter about the restoration of Israel (Isa 49:8–26).³⁰ Pao outlines three stages in the new exodus restoration. These are: "(1) the dawn of salvation

---

23. *Sir* 48:10; Witherington, *Acts,* 110.

24. Menzies, *Development,* 200.

25. Tannehill, *Narrative Unity,* 15–16; Gooding, *True to the Faith,* 41.

26. Johnson, *Acts,* 29; Wall, *Acts,* 42; Peterson, *Acts,* 109. Note also the Lucan emphasis on the restoration of Israel in Luke 2:25, 38; 22:29–30.

27. Sleeman, *Geography and the Ascension Narrative,* 69.

28. Bock, *Proclamation,* 167.

29. Fitzmyer, *Acts,* 206.

30. Turner, *Power,* 300; Menzies, *Development,* 199. The concept of proclamation ἕως ἐσχάτου τῆς γῆς is peculiarly Isaianic coming also in Isa 48:20 and 62:11.

upon Jerusalem; (2) the reconstitution and reunification of Israel [Judea and Samaria] . . . (3) the inclusion of Gentiles within the people of God."[31] Thus, the commission of Acts 1:8 is not only locational but also theopolitical in the restoration of Israel.[32] The restoration of Israel in her new exodus will transcend border controls to encompass all nations under the heavenly Lordship of the risen Christ.

Seventh, another OT allusion is seen in Christ's ascension and reception by a cloud (1:9). Fitzmyer observes that the cloud in the OT was "used in the sense of an apocalyptic stage prop."[33] A number of scholars note parallels with the rapture stories of Enoch,[34] Moses[35] and Elijah.[36] The links with the Elijah narrative are particularly interesting as Elijah's assumption is witnessed by his disciple; that disciple then receives a double portion of his master's spirit; and the same terminology (ἀνελήμφθη (to be taken up); note also the cognate noun ἀναλήμψεως in Luke 9:51) is present (2 Kgs 2:9–11; Luke 9:51; Acts 1:2, 11, 22).[37] Also noted are possible allusions to the cloud of God's presence during the exodus (Exod 16:10; 19:9; 24:15–18).[38] When we recall the association of Moses and Elijah in the transfiguration (Luke 9:30) it seems likely that Luke is presenting Jesus as the prophet like Moses who

---

31. Pao, *Acts and the Isaianic New Exodus*, 95.

32. Ibid.

33. Fitzmyer, *Acts*, 210.

34. Gen 5:21–24; *1 En.* 39:3; *2 En.* 3:1. Johnson, *Acts*, 27.

35. Josephus, *Ant.* IV.viii.48; Philo, *De Vita Mos.* 2:291; Robinson and Wall, *Called to be Church*, 35; Maile, "The Ascension in Luke–Acts," 40.

36. 2 Kings 2:1–18. Brodie, "Luke-Acts as an Imitation and Emulation of the Elijah-Elisha Narrative," 78–85; Pervo, *Acts*, 45. For an outline of all three rapture traditions (that is Enoch, Moses and Elijah) see Zwiep, *The Ascension of the Messiah in Lukan Christology*, 41–76.

37. Talbert, *Reading Acts*, 21; Johnson, *Acts*, 31.

38. Robinson and Wall, *Called to be Church*, 36; Gaventa, *Acts*, 66.

ascends to God in order to receive and then give a new community forming "covenant law".[39]

Eighth, the selection of Matthias to replace Judas reconstitutes the twelve (1:21–26)—a further Lucan allusion to the renewal, reconstitution, and restoration of Israel.[40] With their leader ascended to the Father, and "Israel" waiting below, the administration of the fiery covenant-gift may commence.

All of these allusions together point to a new exodus restoration of Israel. As the narrative progresses we will see a fuller picture of what that restoration looks like and who it now embraces, but at this stage it is important to note that the restoration of Israel as she embarks on her new exodus is an important theme for Luke. Particularly in the early chapters of Acts, Luke is keen to stress that the ascended Christ is still leading his people at a time of monumental redemptive significance.

THE PENTECOST EVENT: ACTS 2:1–15

Although the events of Ascension and Pentecost are separated by several days, thematically and structurally these events are tied together by heavenly activity (1:9; 2:2) and the pattern of prophecy and fulfilment (1:4–8; 2:17–18).[41]

The parallels between the start of Luke's Gospel and Acts are also worthy of our attention here. In both there is a promise of baptism in the Spirit (Luke 3:16; Acts 1:5), followed by the descent

---

39. Cf. also Acts 3:22 and 7:37. By "law" here, I am drawing a connection between the law given at Sinai and the new law written on hearts equated with the Holy Spirit. Jer 31:31–34; Rom 2:29; This will be argued further when we get to Acts 2:33. In Acts 1–2 we see Luke skilfully blending Mosaic, Davidic and Elijah Christologies as Christ is the perfect fulfilment of them all and the end to which they all point (Luke.24:27). Wenk, *Community-Forming Power*, 247.

40. Zwiep, *Judas and the Choice of Matthias*, 159–79; Jervell, *Luke and the People of God*, 75–112; Peterson, *Acts*, 118–20; Wall, *Acts*, 48.

41. Spencer, *Acts*, 33.

of the Spirit (Luke 3:21–22; Acts 2:1–4), then a programmatic sermon (Luke 4:16–30; Acts 2:14–40), followed finally by witness (in words and wonders) to the Jews (Luke 4:31–44; Acts 3–4). These parallels support the special place of the Twelve as Jesus' witnesses, already seen in Acts 1:2–3, 21–26.[42]

There are further new exodus and restoration motifs present in Acts 2 beginning with the Sinai *déjà vu* in Acts 2:1–4.[43] Bock thinks that a "Mosaic background is not significant at all for the Pentecost event."[44] However, there are a number of strands of evidence that suggest a Sinai backdrop to the Pentecost event. First, the Jewish festival of Pentecost is considered by many to have become a remembrance and celebration of the giving of the law at Sinai,[45] and there is some evidence of this in the inter-testamental literature.[46] Second, there are obvious Sinai parallels in the description of the events of 2:1–13. The ascension of Christ to God to receive and dispense the gift parallels Moses' ascension to God to receive the law.[47] Mention of the noise and something like fire coming from heaven provide conceptual parallels to the giving of Torah at

42. Witherington, *Acts*, 128.

43. Spencer, *Acts*, 42.

44. Bock, *Proclamation*, 182–83; So too Barrett, *Acts*, 111–12. It must be said that Bock seems more sympathetic to a Mosaic background in his later commentary, *Acts*, 95–96.

45. Talbert, *Acts*, 41; Parsons, *Acts*, 36; Spencer, *Acts*, 42; Betz, "φωνή," 296.

46. *Jub*. 1:1; 6:17–19; 14:20 associates covenant renewal with Pentecost (feast of weeks); See Vermes, *The Dead Sea Scrolls*, 177–78. Further support would be gained if Luke knew of Philo's description of the law-giving at Sinai which included descending fire and utter amazement at a voice which spoke in language familiar to them. The linguistic parallels in the Greek are striking (Philo, *Decal*. 46). With regards to the *Jubilees* references, Barrett, arguing against Sinai allusions, notes that *Jub*. 6:17–19 links the feast only to God's covenant with Noah (Barrett, *Acts 1–14*, 111). However, *Jub*. 14:20 links the renewal of the festival with the Abrahamic covenant. It is not a leap too far to see a development which connected the feast more broadly with God's covenants with his people.

47. Beale, "The Descent," 81.

Sinai (Ex 19:18–20).[48] Menzies here considers the differences in the accounts to outweigh any similarities and considers the features to be the common currency of theophanic traditions.[49] However, Sinai remains a foundational theophany,[50] and, as Johnson points out, "nowhere is the same cluster of symbols found all together except in the Septuagint's description of Sinai."[51] Third, there are linguistic parallels between Acts 2 and Exodus 19–20. These are as follows: ὁμοῦ (together; Acts 2:1) or its synonym ὁμοθυμαδὸν (Exod 19:8; Acts 1:14; 2:46); φωνῆ (sound; Exod 19:16; Acts 2:6); and ἐκ τοῦ οὐρανοῦ (from heaven; Exod 20:22; Acts 2:2).[52] These strands of evidence together provide a cumulative case for seeing Pentecost being portrayed as a new Sinai. Further, the use of ekphrastic language underscores the significance of the event for the ensuing narrative.[53]

Having been filled with the Spirit (1:5; 2:3), the disciples begin to speak (1:8; 2:4). Turner describes the tongues-speech as an example of invasive charismatic praise,[54] but is there more to it here? Jordan argues that the tongues-speech is a sign of judgment against Israel as the gospel is now going to be offered to Gentiles,[55] but this overlooks the fact that those gathered are Jews of the diaspora who hear in their own dialects, and the gospel will go out to the Jews with great power and effect over subsequent chapters of Acts. Menzies, by contrast, argues that the tongues-speech was-

---

48. Peterson, *Acts*, 131. See also Bock, *Acts*, 97–98; Parsons, *Acts*, 36; Maxwell, *Hearing Between the Lines*, 151–52.

49. Menzies, *Development*, 235–41.

50. Pervo, *Acts*, 61.

51. Johnson, *Acts*, 46.

52. Fitzmyer, *Acts*, 234.

53. Parsons, *Acts*, 38. Ekphrasis is the use of vivid or colourful imagery to heighten the rhetorical effect.

54. Turner, *Power*, 271.

55. Jordan, *Through New Eyes*, 275. If there is a judgment motif present it may more likely be one of judgement on the Jews of Jerusalem who rejected and killed their Messiah. See Weatherly, *Jewish Responsibility*, 175.

for missionary purposes.[56] It is certainly clear that the following speech contains an appeal for repentance and faith, and the events allude to missional prophecies (Isa 11:11–12; 49:6). However, it seems unlikely that the tongues-speech was primarily for missional means. The two other occurrences of tongues-speech within Acts have no other outsiders present (10:46; 19:6).[57] Menzies is also speculating as to the content of the μεγαλεῖα τοῦ θεοῦ (the wonders of God).[58] A more nuanced approach is to see tongues-speech as a logical sign of the *purpose* of Spirit-baptism—to witness to the ends of the earth.[59]

There is also something else alluded to here with the tongues-speech. Many scholars see here an allusion to the story of the Tower of Babel in Genesis 11.[60] At Babel languages are confused and people scattered in judgement; at Pentecost languages are un-

---

56. Menzies, *Development*, 211.

57. Turner, *Power*, 272. These other occurrences in Acts (10:46; 19:6) also rule out Zerhusen's proposal that in Acts 2 the disciples are simply speaking ordinary Greek instead of Hebrew which would have been a shock to hearers. If this were the case there would be no need to draw attention to the examples in 10:46 and 19:6. Zerhusen, "An Overlooked Diglossia in Acts 2?" 118–30. Zerhusen is responding to a perceived problem which does not exist. Although Jews of the diaspora would have all spoken Greek, there would also have been regional dialects and accents as pointed out by Meeks, *The First Urban Christians*, 15.

58. Green points out that the missionary proclamation does not begin until v. 14. Until then the disciples are extolling God. Green, "In Our Own Languages," 202. Peterson suggests from the content of Peter's sermon (vv. 16–39) that they were speaking of Jesus' exaltation. This may be right but is un-provable. Peterson, *Acts*, 137. Old Testament and inter-testamental literature most frequently speaks of God's μεγαλεῖα with reference to his deeds of deliverance (Deut 11:2; Ps 70:19; *Tob* 11:15; *2 Macc* 3:34; 7:17; *3 Macc* 7:22; *Sir* 17:8, 10, 13; 18:4; 36:7; 42:21; 43:15; 45:24).

59. Keener, "Why Does Luke Use Tongues as a Sign of the Spirit's Empowerment?" 182–84. Keener describes the sign of tongues as a "proleptic foreshadowing of the 'Gentile Mission.'"

60. Barrett, *Acts*, 112; Gilbert, "From Eschatology to Imperialism," 95; Scott, "Luke's Geographical Horizon," 520–38; Keener, "Why Does Luke Use Tongues," 181; Parsons, Acts 39–40.

derstood and people bought together as a foretaste of what this new salvation would look like as the curse of Babel is reversed. In support of this there are linguistic as well as conceptual parallels: γλῶσσα (tongues; Gen 11:7; Acts 2:3, 4, 11); ἕκαστος (each; Gen 11:7; Acts 2:8); ἀκούω (to hear; Gen 11:7; Acts 2:8). That is not to downplay the Sinai motif but rather to add another layer to Luke's rich tapestry. If there is a sense in which Babel is reversed this would further support the restoration motif already argued for as nations stream to Jerusalem (Mic 4:1–2).[61] A reversal, recapitulation or even parody of Babel fits with the view that the list of nations in 2:9–11 has some relationship to the table of nations in Gen 10.[62] Those once divided are now being united as those "under heaven" (Acts 2:5).

There are various interpretations regarding the meaning of the list of nations in 2:9–11. Interpreters consider the list of nations to be: a random list;[63] representative of universality;[64] representative of the table of nations in Genesis 10;[65] a political statement.[66] The first option is unlikely given Luke's care with his account—in particular the careful geographical ordering of the list. The last three options are more plausible and, I suggest, together give the answer. We are told in Acts 2:5 that men had gathered from "every nation under heaven." Heaven, in Acts, is the place from which the

---

61. For links between Micah and Isaiah, and the theme of restoration in Micah see Stansell, *Micah and Isaiah*, 39–66.

62. Green argues that Pentecost is a parody of Babel as diverse languages are bought together not for preservation from scattering (Gen 11:4) but for the purpose of scattering. Green, "In Our Own Languages," 208–13.

63. Fitzmyer, *Acts*, 240.

64. Spencer, *Acts*, 44. He considers the list is descriptive of the four corners of the earth. See also Marshall, *Acts*, 71. Metzger argues that the list represents universality under the twelve signs of the zodiac, but the connections are unconvincing. Metzger, "Ancient Astrological Geography," 123–133.

65. Parsons, *Acts*, 39–40. Scott, "Luke's Geographical Horizon," 530. This understanding might fit particularly well if Pentecost is understood as a reversal of Babel.

66. Gilbert, "From Eschatology to Imperialism," 84–110.

Acts 2:17-21 Within the Context of Acts 1-2

risen and ascended Christ exercises his universal rule. In terms of Gen 10, the linguistic connections between Acts 2 and Gen 11 extend back to Gen 10 (γλῶσσά—tongues; Gen 10:5, 20, 31). Genesis 10 also gives us a list of all the nations under the heavenly rule of YHWH. And politically, just as the writer of Genesis lists the nations of the earth under YHWH, so too ancient Rome had a practice of listing the nations of the earth under Caesar.[67] Luke then is making a theopolitical statement by reconstituting the nations under heaven—that is, under *Christ's* rule,[68] as well as perhaps drawing on OT prophecies about the ingathering of the exiles (Isa 11:11-12; Acts 2:5-11).[69] Again, the imagery connotes restoration and new exodus motifs.

THE EXPLANATION: ACTS 2:16-40

The speech explains the events just witnessed by the crowd in terms of the resurrection, ascension and exaltation of the Messiah, Jesus.[70] The purpose of citing Joel 3:1-5 (LXX) is clear—it explains the prophetic events just witnessed by the masses. But it goes beyond a justification for the events themselves to set up a proclamation of the heavenly author of the events.

Immediately after the Joel citation, Peter accredits wonders and signs (τέρασι καὶ σημείοις) to Jesus in 2:22, demonstrating the Christological application of the quotation—the miraculous as

---

67. This in fact is similar to the argument Gilbert makes, linking Gen 10-11, Acts 2, and the political propaganda of Luke's day. Luke's point is theopolitical. Gilbert, "From Eschatology to Imperialism," 94-95.

68. There may also be a movement through time as well as space as the empires listed span the Parthians to the Romans. This may further highlight Christ's superiority over Caesar. See Nasrallah, "The Acts of the Apostles, Greek Cities, and Hadrian's Panhellenion," 557.

69. Pao, *Acts,* 130-31. We also must remember the strong influence the Gen 10 table of nations exerts on the OT and other Jewish literature. See Scott, "Luke's Geographical Horizon," 520.

70. *Contra* Barrett who inexplicably deems the speech to have nothing in it to connect it with the occasion. Barrett, *Acts 1-14,* 133.

authenticating is constitutive of Lucan Christology.[71] The phrase "τέρασι καὶ σημείοις" is the first of several instances of links between the Joel quotation and the rest of the speech.[72] The connection between "signs and wonders" and the events of the exodus have already been noted in chapter 1.

Peter moves from Jesus' life to his foreordained death and on to his resurrection. The quotation from Psalm 16 (LXX 15):8–11, cited in vv. 25–28, demonstrates that the resurrection of Jesus, witnessed by his disciples, is the vindication of him as the "Holy One" of God. Jesus is shown to be the Messiah and David's eschatological heir.[73] Notes of restoration again resound as a Davidic King is returned to the throne (v. 30) in fulfilment of the OT hope seen in places like 2 Sam 7:12–13; 1 Kgs 11:36, 39; Ezek 37:24–25; Hos 3:5; and Amos 9:11. This is a key aspect of Luke's soteriological enterprise (see Acts 15:16).[74]

Here we begin to see how "exodus" and "restoration" themes converge. When we recall that there had not been a King on David's throne since the exile we can see why the Jews still considered themselves in exile.[75] A new exodus provides both liberation and restoration simultaneously. With the throne occupied and the covenant ratified, liberation and restoration can begin, and have in fact already begun (vv. 30–33). Turner suggests that as we get to Jesus' exaltation (vv. 33–36) we have a fusion of "Davidic and

---

71. See also Luke 4:36; 19:37. Fitzmyer, *Acts*, 20.

72. See also ἐκχεῶ (to pour out—2:17, 18, 33); κύριος (Lord—2:21, 25, 34, 36, 39); and ὄνομα (name—2:21, 38). Bock also suggests some other possible word links under the *gezerah shewa* technique. See Bock, *Acts*, 134. See also Longenecker, *Acts*, 279.

73. Turner, *Power from on High*, 275.

74. Lee, "Evangelical Dialogue," 87.

75. Judah had of course had self-acclaimed priest-kings in the Hasmonean dynasty, and puppet kings in the Herodian, but Davidic kings these were not. For evidence of early Jews viewing themselves as still in exile see *Sir* 36; *Bar* 2:7–10; *Tob* 13:5; *2 Macc* 2:18; *1 En* 89; *Test Mos* 4:8–9; see also Wright, *The New Testament and the People of God*, 157–61; 268–69.

Mosaic Christologies together in a new exodus soteriology."[76] The argument is built partly on seeing an allusion in v. 33 to the Jewish Targum on Ps 68:19 (MT) which interprets the verse as referring to the giving of the law at Sinai.[77] The Targum on Ps 68:19 (MT) reads:

> You have ascended to the firmament, O prophet Moses, you took captives, you taught the words of the Law, you gave them as gifts to the sons of man[78]

While rabbinic exegesis of the Psalm celebrates the gift of the Law through the ascended Moses, now it is fulfilled in the gift of the Spirit through the ascended Christ.[79] It is the figures of David and Moses *together* who play the part here.[80]

The use of δεξιᾷ (right side) in v. 33 leads into the quotation from Ps 109:1 (LXX).[81] Citing Ps 109:1 (LXX) demonstrates that this risen and exalted Messiah has taken his place at the right hand of God as both Lord and Christ. The final appeal to the audience takes us back to Joel 3:1–5 (LXX) with mention of the "name" (now clearly identified as Jesus Christ) and the promise of the Spirit. The promise in Acts 2:29 is said to be "for you, your children and all who are far off" echoing another promise of covenant renewal and restoration in Isa 59:19–21.[82] The final appeal in Acts 2:40 to be saved from this crooked and perverse generation (τῆς γενεᾶς τῆς σκολιᾶς ταύτης) once again alludes to the wilderness generation

---

76. Turner, *Power*, 279. I have already argued above that the fusion also includes an Elijah Christology seen in the ascension.

77. See also Dupont, "Ascension du Christ et don de l'Esprit d'après Actes 2:33," 229.

78. Stec, *The Targum of Psalms*, 131.

79. Dupont, "Ascension," 229 *pace* Marshall who sees the proposal as doubtful. *Acts*, 79.

80. Turner, *Power*, 289; So also Peterson, *Acts*, 151.

81. Johnson, *Acts*, 52.

82. Ruthven, "This is My Covenant With Them" 232. While I agree with Ruthven that Acts 2:39 alludes to Isa 59:19–21, I find his proposal of the Isaiah text as programmatic for the wider Acts narrative less convincing.

THE POWER OF PENTECOST

which Moses addressed in Deut 32:5 (γενεὰ σκολιά; also in Ps 77:8 with reference to the wilderness generation). This Davidic Christ is ruling over his restored covenant people, with his Spirit being the evidential stamp on his people of his rule. Just as Caesar's face on coinage was evidence of his rule, so the Holy Spirit is the living personal evidence that Jesus reigns.[83]

CONCLUSION

Even if one does not accept every OT allusion proposed, the weight of the paradigm is difficult to resist. It seems beyond doubt that Luke is deliberately portraying these events as a new exodus in the restoration of Israel.[84]

In summary, Acts 1–2 presents the reader with a programme of restoration. The forty days, teaching about the Kingdom, the promised commissioning and clothing with power, the ascension, and the reconstitution of the Twelve all echo OT liberation and restoration motifs. The events of Acts 2:1–13 represent Pentecost as a new Sinai, a re-gathering of God's people under Christ's rule, receiving a constitutive gift. The explanation of Acts 2:14–39 further demonstrates the Christological nature of the events. The

---

83. We could go on at this point to consider the way in which the new community, described in Acts 2:42–47, bore witness to God's restorative work. Mention of signs and wonders again alludes to the exodus generation, while winning "the favour of all the people" is a conceptual echo of Deut 4:5–8. The promise of Joel (2:21) is fulfilled in 2:47 as many are being saved.

84. In addition to the OT allusions already posited, Evans has noted that Acts 2 is "laced with language taken from Joel." He notes twenty word matches between Acts 2 and the book of Joel. Evans suggests significant echoes include μεθύω (to be drunk—Joel 1:5; Acts 2:15), which occurs five times in the NT; συγχέω (to be confused—Joel 2:1,10; Acts 2:6) occurring four times in the NT; and ἐνωτίζομαι (to listen/give ear—Joel 1:2; Acts 2:14) which is a NT hapax. Evans, "The Prophetic Setting of the Pentecost Sermon," 148–50. When we remember that restoration is a significant theme within the book of Joel this lends further support to the theme of restoration as being key for Luke. For restoration as a key theme in Joel see Stuart, *Hosea-Jonah*, 228–31; McQueen, *Joel and the Spirit*, 38–43; Wolff, *Joel and Amos*, 12–14; VanGemeren, "The Spirit of Restoration," 81–102.

Davidic King has been raised to life and exalted to the throne from which he administers his executive rule through his Spirit. Turner observes that Jesus is the "Son of David", the Davidic King who ascends to his heavenly throne "decked out in Mosaic regalia and with a Sinai chorus."[85]

To state the obvious, this means that the Joel quotation has a context within Acts. It does not exist in isolation—its meaning and application must be derived from situating it within its wider context. Pentecost is "viewed as part of the fulfilment and *renewal* of Israel's covenant, and so . . . the gift of the Spirit will have a vital role in Israel's restoration."[86] We must remember that there is something uniquely constitutive about the Pentecost event and its explanation in 2:17–21. Like the first exodus, this new exodus, liberating slaves and forming a new Israel, is a significant redemptive historical moment.[87]

The relationship of these new exodus events to subsequent generations is a complex question. Should we consider these things paradigmatic since all are caught up in the last days?[88] Or, is the relationship more akin to that of the "Deuteronomy generation" who are closely associated with the events of the Exodus without being physically present?[89]

There is certainly something constitutive about these events, yet the Spirit's liberation transcends temporal and spatial boundaries to incorporate all who call on the name of the Lord in the last days. Thus while there is something exceptional about the first Pentecost and exodus-like restoration of Israel, it is difficult to argue that the phenomena related to the promise are *never* to be experienced again by subsequent generations of believers. Whatever our understanding of Acts 2:17–21 in the wider char-

---

85. Turner, *Power*, 279.
86. Ibid., 289.
87. Hays, "The Liberation of Israel in Luke-Acts," 101–117.
88. Menzies, "Acts 2:17–21," 200–218.
89. See Deut 1:26–33; 4:10–14, 35–36.

ismatic debates, we must first understand it in the context of Acts 1–2. Having refined our understanding of Acts 2:17–21 in light of Acts 1–2, we now need to understand how the prophecy functions in the subsequent narrative. This leads us into the next stage of our enquiry.

3

Acts 2:17–21 Within the Subsequent Narrative of Acts

INTRODUCTION

HAVING EXAMINED Acts 2:17–21 independently and in relation to the rest of Acts 1–2, we move to consider what role the text plays in the ensuing narrative. Many have noted the programmatic nature of Peter's Pentecost speech on the subsequent narrative. That is not to deny Acts 1:8 programmatic status but rather to suggest that Acts 2:17–21 is epexegetical of Acts 1:8. Turner, for example, states, "Peter's explanation of the Pentecost event in Acts 2:14–39 has perhaps greater claim than Luke 4:16–30 to be called "the programmatic" text of Luke–Acts."[1] Tannehill also notes that "major portions of the Joel quotation are "active" in the surrounding text of Acts, which narrates the progressive fulfilment of the divine promises in Joel."[2] We shall trace each element in turn, considering its presence and part in the subsequent narrative.

TONGUES-SPEECH

Strictly speaking, tongues are not part of the promise of Acts 2:17–21. However, since we observed earlier that the prophecy spoken of in 2:18 is linked to the tongues-speech just witnessed, it seems

---

1. Turner, *Power*, 267.
2. Tannehill, *Narrative Unity*, 32.

appropriate to consider further evidences of the phenomenon in the ensuing narrative.³

Speaking in tongues occurs in two other places in the book of Acts—10:46 and 19:6. The final part of chapter 10 is structured to convey something of a Gentile Pentecost.⁴ There are numerous linguistic parallels with the events of Acts 2 as follows:

i. λαλεῖν ἑτέραις γλώσσαις (to speak other languages; 2:4) and λαλούντων γλώσσαις (10:46);

ii. μεγαλεῖα τοῦ θεοῦ (the wonders of God; 2:11) and μεγαλυνόντων τὸν θεόν (10:46);⁵

iii. ἐκχεῶ (pour out; 2:17,18), ἐξέχεεν (2:33), and ἐκκέχυται (10:45);

iv. βαπτισθήτω ἕκαστος ὑμῶν ἐπὶ τῷ ὀνόματι Ἰησοῦ Χριστου (Let each of you be baptized in the name of Jesus Christ; 2:38) and ἐν τῷ ὀνόματι Ἰησοῦ Χριστοῦ βαπτισθῆναι (10:48);

v. Ἰωάννης μὲν ἐβάπτισεν ὕδατί ὑμεῖς δὲ ἐν πνεύματι βαπτισθήσεσθε ἁγίῳ (John baptized you with water but you will be baptized in the Holy Spirit; 1:5; 11:16 with some change in word order).⁶

Further, the amount of narrative space given to this episode in Acts 10–11 indicates the significance of Cornelius' (and his household's) conversion.⁷ It has to be seen in the same order of magnitude as Pentecost for the early Jewish church to accept these

3. In chapter one of this book we argued that since Peter quotes Joel as an *apologia* for the phenomena of tongues-speech just witnessed, and given the only word-gift mentioned in the Joel quotation is prophecy, we should see tongues speaking as a subset of the wider category of prophecy. This will be further developed below.

4. Bruce, *Acts,* 264; Bock, *Acts,* 400.

5. This parallel is noted by Behm, "γλῶσσα," 724.

6. See also Richard, "Pentecost as a Recurrent Theme in Luke-Acts," 137–139.

7. In addition the Cornelius episode is spoken of by Peter in the crucial events of Acts 15 (see Acts 15:7–11), further highlighting its importance.

Acts 2:17-21 Within the Subsequent Narrative of Acts

Gentile believers.[8] Speaking in tongues is the audible legitimation for such acceptance as Peter makes clear in Acts 11:15-17.[9] Similarly, Acts 19:1-7 presents glossolalia as evidence of initiation. Again, there are some verbal echoes from Acts 1-2:

i. ἐβαπτίσθησαν εἰς τὸ ὄνομα τοῦ κυρίου Ἰησοῦ (they were baptized into the name of the Lord Jesus; 19:5; cf. 2:38);

ii. ἦλθε τὸ πνεῦμα τὸ ἅγιον ἐπ' αὐτούς (the holy Spirit came upon them; 19:6; cf. 1:8);

iii. ἐλάλουν τε γλώσσαις καὶ ἐπροφήτευον (they began to speak in languages and prophesy; 19:6; cf. 2:4, 17-18).

The disciples in Ephesus had been baptised with John's baptism.[10] They were not aware that the Holy Spirit had already been poured out, and thus their tongues-speech is evidence of genuine conversion. Before receiving the Spirit they are John's disciples, not Jesus'. While some scholars consider the Ephesian disciples to be Christians, I do not for the following reasons: First, Witherington notes this is the only place in Acts where μαθητὰς (disciples) is used without the definite article.[11] Second, it seems unlikely that disciples of Jesus could be unsure whether the Holy Spirit had come.[12] Third, Spirit reception is, in Witherington's words, the "*sine qua non* of being a Christian" as seems to be clear from Acts 11:17.[13] Finally, this is the only instance of re-baptism in Acts suggesting they were not yet Jesus' disciples.[14] It would be very strange if Jesus'

8. Bruce describes Peter's actions as "epoch-making." Bruce, *Acts*, 265.
9. Parsons, *Acts*, 156.
10. The preparatory nature of John's baptism is stressed by the fronting of εἰς τὸν ἐρχόμενον μετ' αὐτὸν before ἵνα. Bruce, *Acts*, 407.
11. Witherington, *Acts*, 570-72.
12. This is based on translating ἀλλ' οὐδ' εἰ πνεῦμα ἅγιον ἔστιν ἠκούσαμεν in v. 2 as "but we have not heard if the Holy Spirit is [come]."
13. Witherington, *Acts*, 570-72.
14. For other scholars in agreement with Witherington see Peterson, *Acts*, 529-31; Marshall, *Acts*, 305; Käsemann, "The Disciples of John the Baptist," 136. For those who do consider the Ephesian disciples to have been Christians

41

disciples need to be re-baptised into his name. It is preferable to view the Ephesian disciples of John being in the uniquely liminal position of living as what might be described as Old Testament believers post Christ. They experience, what Fitzmyer terms, the "Pentecost of Johannine Christians."[15] This is the final mention of tongues-speech in Acts and perhaps serves as the Paul parallel to the earlier story of Peter and John (8:14–17).[16] In Acts 2, 10 and 19 we have historically unique situations—Pentecost, the first Gentile converts, and the last Old Testament believers.[17]

At this point it is worth commenting on the doctrine of subsequence—that is the belief within Pentecostalism that reception of the Spirit can be separated from conversion, with tongues-speech being the initial evidence of Spirit reception. Support for this is often adduced from texts such as Acts 2, 8, 10 and 19.[18] As has been argued, Acts 19 does not provide evidence for the Holy Spirit being a *donum superadditum*. On the contrary, Acts 19 clearly portrays those involved as yet unconverted until Paul evangelizes them.[19] Acts 8 occupies a similar social context as Acts 10. When one understands the depth of feeling, and the racial and religious

---

see Menzies, *Development*, 271–77; Bruce, *Acts*, 406.

15. Fitzmyer, *Acts*, 644.

16. Bock, *Acts*, 600. Johnson considers the tongues-speech to legitimate both the believers and the apostle. Johnson, *Acts*, 338.

17. Some may wish to see the Ethiopian eunuch as the first Gentile convert, but Cornelius is significant as the first "first-space" convert (see Sleeman, *Geography and the Ascension Narrative*, 224). The Ethiopian eunuch disappears from view as he goes on his way at the end of Acts 8. Cornelius and his household however, are permanently localized. With regards to Acts 19, Carson describes the Ephesian believers as still belonging to the "old era," and Peterson describes them as a transitional group in salvation-historical terms. Carson, *Showing the Spirit*, 150; Peterson, *Acts*, 533.

18. Scholars arguing for tongues as initial evidence from such texts include Bruner, *A Theology of the Holy Spirit*, 76; Petts, "The Baptism in the Holy Spirit," 107. Although tongues are not mentioned in Acts 8 a number of scholars consider this would have been the visible manifestation of Spirit reception as in 2:4; 10:46; and 19:6. See Bock, *Acts*, 332; Bruce, *Acts*, 222.

19. Dunn, *Baptism*, 83–89 *contra* Stronstad, *Charismatic Theology*, 68–69.

Acts 2:17-21 Within the Subsequent Narrative of Acts

tension that existed between Jews and Samaritans, one can see the necessity of the presence of the apostles in verifying the conversion of Samaritans.[20] The very necessity of apostolic presence indicates that the situation is far from normal. This is the first reported occurrence of the Spirit being given outside of Jerusalem.[21] The spread to Samaria is further evidence of the reconstitution of Israel. Therefore Acts 8 cannot be considered paradigmatic for Christian experience in subsequent generations.[22] Further, there is no uniform presentation of an *ordo salutis* in Acts.[23] In Acts 2:38 the promise is that all who repent and are baptized will receive the promised Spirit. In Acts 8 there is a delay between belief, baptism and then the reception of the Spirit. In Acts 10 the Spirit falls as Peter is speaking and the baptism follows. In Acts 19 baptism precedes Spirit reception. Part of the explanation is that repentance, faith, baptism and Spirit-reception are a complex of events that occur, to some degree, contemporaneously, and each assumes the presence of the others.[24] When that is not the case, it is considered unusual and therefore warrants comment. It is also worth bearing in mind the distinction between the animistic and dynamic fillings of the Spirit observed by Schweizer.[25] To affirm that "animistic" fillings are possible is not to affirm the possibility of being converted without the Spirit.

---

20. Witherington, *Acts*, 289; Peterson, *Acts*, 287; Bock, *Acts*, 330; Lee, "Evangelical Dialogue," 89-90; *contra* Fitzmyer who considers the gift of the Spirit to only come through apostles or late, apostolic delegates. Fitzmyer, *Acts*, 400. For the relationship between Jews and Samaritans see John 4:9; Josephus, *Ant.* ix. 291; xi. 340-42; Goodman, *Rome and Jerusalem*, 175-76.

21. Barrett, *Acts 1-14*, 413.

22. Peterson, *Acts*, 287.

23. Schweizer, *Holy Spirit*, 62.

24. Note baptism is linked with washing in a regenerative or sanctifying way in Acts 22:16.

25. See chapter one. Schweizer, "πνεῦμα," 407-9.

THE POWER OF PENTECOST

In summary, tongues-speech within Acts serves a socio-ecclesiological function.[26] Tongues-speech serves to demonstrate to outsiders (Acts 2) and insiders (Acts 10, 19) who it is that now constitutes the people of God.[27] Luke demonstrates the fulfilment of Joel 3:1–5 (LXX) through recurrent "Pentecosts" within the narrative.[28] Such initial evidence cannot be considered normative or prescriptive given Luke's presentation in which tongues-speech serves to legitimate controversial people-groups.[29]

PROPHECY

Prophesy of course consists of more than just tongues-speech as is evidenced from its occurrences in the rest of Acts. The verb, προφητεύω, only occurs once in the rest of Acts with reference to the new believers in Ephesus (19:6) where the utterance appears to be spontaneous, though the content is not provided. The noun, προφήτης, occurs with reference to NT prophets five times in Acts (11:27; 13:1; 15:32; 21:9, 10).[30] One of the questions to address here is whether our understanding of prophecy should be limited to those instances where the word itself (προφήτης/προφητεύω) appears or whether we should read prophecy into a broader range of

---

26. Carson notes that never in Acts is tongues the experience of an isolated individual—it is always a corporate activity. Carson, *Showing the Spirit*, 145.

27. And by implication those who do not (in the case of disciples of John the Baptist). "The Spirit is apologetically employed to verify that the Ephesian Baptist's disciples are to be incorporated into the people of God, as previously in relation to the Samaritans (Acts 8:14–17) and Cornelius' (Gentile) household (Acts 10:44–48)." Hur, *A Dynamic Reading of the Holy Spirit in Luke-Acts*, 260.

28. Stott says they "experienced a mini-Pentecost. Better, Pentecost caught up on them." Stott, *Acts*, 305.

29. Turner, *Power*, 392–94.

30. I am including Philip's daughters (Acts 21:9) in the noun list although technically they are identified using a substantival participle—προφητεύουσαι. The noun, prophecy, appears thirty times in Acts, but the overwhelming majority of those occurrences refer to OT prophets, and three refer to Jesus (3:22, 23; 7:37).

activities—charismatic preaching, praying, or words of rebuke for example.

Some argue that where we observe instances of Spirit-filled preaching, or the Spirit communicating to people, we should not equate that with prophecy. Rather, they should be viewed as inspired preaching or teaching,[31] or, in the case of the Spirit speaking, a "strong subjective sense of guidance."[32] For example, Grudem, commenting on the setting apart of Barnabas and Paul (Acts 13:2), states, "Luke's failure to attribute the speech to any one of the prophets, coupled with his pattern elsewhere of attributing *non-prophetic* speech to the Holy Spirit, make it somewhat doubtful that prophecy is in view here."[33]

However, the following evidence suggests Luke *does* consider Spirit-inspired speech to be prophecy. First, Luke portrays the Spirit as a key figure in both his first and second volumes;[34] the Spirit is pre-eminently the speaking Spirit—indeed, the Spirit of prophecy.[35] As the Spirit is one who speaks, so also he equips others to speak (Luke 12:11–12; Acts 1:8). Second, there is a connection between the Spirit and those who are explicitly identified as prophets in the narrative. Agabus, identified as a prophet in 11:28, is said to speak διὰ τοῦ πνεύματος (through the Spirit; 11:28). David is also said to have spoken διὰ πνεύματος ἁγίου (4:25) and is identified as a prophet in 2:30. The Spirit is also said to have spoken through (διὰ) Isaiah in Acts 28:25. There we have three clear examples of prophets who are either said to speak through the Spirit, or the Spirit is said to speak through them.[36] Therefore,

31. Turner, *The Holy Spirit and Spiritual Gifts*, 206–12.
32. Grudem, *The Gift of Prophecy*, 73–74.
33. Ibid.
34. Luke 1:17, 41, 67; 3:22; 4:1; 4:14; 10:21; 11:13; 12:12. Acts 1:4–5, 8; 2:1–4; 4:8; 5:32; 6:5; 7:55; 8:15, 29; 9:31; 10:19, 44; 11:12, 15, 28; 13:2, 4, 9; 15:8, 28; 19:6; 20:22; 21:11; 28:25.
35. Acts 1:16; 4:25; 5:32; 6:10; 8:29; 10:19; 11:12; 11:28; 13:2; 13:9; 20:23; 21:4; 21:11; 28:25. See Turner, "The Spirit of Prophecy," 327–48.
36. We might also add Zechariah who is filled with the Holy Spirit and

when the speaking Spirit communicates, fills, or comes upon believers, and they in turn speak Spirit-inspired words, we should consider that to be prophecy. That is not to say that whenever we hear of the Spirit speaking we equate that with prophecy, but rather, when the Spirit fills or communicates, and a human agent in turn speaks, we should regard that as prophecy.

From this it follows that there is a range of forms and functions that constitute prophecy. First, prophecy may be predictive. We see this most clearly in the case of Agabus who predicts a famine in 11:27–28, and Paul's arrest in 21:11.[37]

Second, prophecy may be a spoken revelation, through the Spirit; for example, the setting apart of Barnabas and Saul, which presumably happened through a human orator (13:1–2),[38] or the warnings given to Paul in 21:4.[39]

Third, the new believers of Ephesus in 19:6 appear to be exercising a simultaneously ecstatic, spontaneous and evidential form of prophecy. There is a close connection in this instance between

---

prophesies in Luke 1:67. Johnson says that the phrase "filled with the Spirit" is Luke's "stereotypical characterization of his main characters as prophets, both in the Gospel (1:15, 41, 67; 4:1) and in Acts (2:4; 4:31; 6:3, 5; 7:55; 9:17; 11:24; 13:9)." Johnson, *Acts*, 77.

37. Grudem and Witherington argue from Acts 21:11 that NT prophecy differs from OT prophecy in terms of accuracy and authority, needing to be weighed and sifted (1 Cor 14:29). Grudem, *The Gift of Prophecy*, 77–83; Witherington, *Acts*, 630–31. Carson, commenting on Acts 21:11 states, "I can think of no reported Old Testament prophet whose prophecies are so wrong on the details." Carson, *Showing the Spirit*, 97–98. However, Bock says the prophecy should not be pressed too literally and is broadly accurate. Bock, *Acts*, 638. Peterson also suggests that the prophecy is broadly correct and helpfully notes that Paul himself looks back on the event in Acts 28:17 and says "I was arrested in Jerusalem and handed over to the Romans." Peterson, *Acts*, 580. This would indicate that Paul considers Agabus' prophecy to have been correct. Even if we consider Agabus to be in line with OT prophets, I still think, based on the argument outlined, that within Acts prophecy covers a broad range of activity.

38. Aune, *Prophecy in Early Christianity*, 192; Barrett, *Acts 1–14*, 605; Bruce, *Acts*, 294.

39. Witherington, *Acts*, 392, 630.

tongues-speech and prophesy (as in Acts 2) and this ecstatic prophecy is reminiscent of some OT prophecy (1 Sam 10:5; 19:8).[40]

Fourth, prophecy is connected with encouragement and exhortation.[41] See for example Judas and Silas, described as prophets who "encouraged and strengthened the brothers with many words" (15:32).[42] Their identification as prophets is not to give credibility—that is established in 15:22 where the men are designated leaders. Their designation as prophets puts them in the same company as Paul and Barnabas, and is related to the content of their "encouraging" and "strengthening" speech.

Fifth, various commentators see bold Spirit-inspired witness/preaching as prophecy, such as happens in 2:14–40;[43] 3:12–26; 4:8–12;[44] 5:29–32.[45] This should be unsurprising since in 1:8 Jesus promises his disciples they would be empowered to witness when the Spirit came upon them. Then, when the Spirit comes, Peter cites Joel 3:1–5 (LXX). The only oral witness gift spoken of there is prophecy. In the ensuing narrative we see disciples, once cowed with fear (cf. Luke. 24:37), now witnessing boldly (Acts 4:13). It is not a step too far for the reader to consider such Spirit-empowered speech as prophecy.[46]

Sixth, there appears to be an association between prophecy and teaching.[47] Barnabas and Paul are described as teaching in

40. Friedrich and Meyer, "προφήτης," 797, 852.

41. Brown and Peisker, "Prophet" 87; Aune, *Prophecy,* 192; Gaffin describes this as the "hortatory" function of prophecy. Gaffin, *Perspectives on Pentecost,* 67.

42. ESV. Peterson views the ministry of Judas and Silas in Acts 15:32 as prophetic. Peterson, *Acts,* 441; So too Fitzmyer, *Acts,* 568; Bruce, *Acts,* 348.

43. Peterson, *Acts,* 139; Johnson, *Acts,* 53–54.

44. Fitzmyer, *Acts,* 300; Witherington, *Acts,* 193. Acts 4:8 along with 4:31 are examples of the animistic filling described by Schweizer (*TDNT* 6:407–09). Disciples receive a "filling" to empower them for witness. Peterson, *Acts,* 190.

45. Fitzmyer, *Acts,* 338; Menzies, "Acts 2:17–21," 209–10.

46. See the argument given in Menzies, "Acts 2:17–21," 209–210.

47. Friedrich and Meyer, "προφήτης," 854.

Antioch in 11:26 (immediately prior to the visit of the Jerusalem prophets in 11:27–31) and when Luke picks up again in Antioch at 13:1 we learn about a church of "prophets and teachers." That is not to say they are identical, but rather that the distinction is not sharp.[48]

Seventh, we see Paul deliver a Spirit-inspired judgement oracle against Elymas in 13:9–11.[49]

Thus, prophecy in its variegated richness is seen throughout the narrative in fulfilment of Joel's promise that all would prophesy. Bruce points out that prophecy was widely considered to have ceased in the inter-testamental period, with its reappearance in the ministry of John the Baptist (Luke 3:2; 7:26f), Jesus (Luke 7:16; 24:19; Acts 3:22), and now the apostles, testifying to the restoration of Israel.[50] Certain characters (particularly Peter and Paul as apostles) are to the fore, and while "all" could prophesy (Acts 2:17–18), some are especially gifted to it, such as Agabus (in terms of prediction; Acts 11:27–28), or Judas and Silas (in terms of encouragement; Acts 15:30–32).[51] We do still see however, that there is a range of people and functions involved. As argued above, prophecy covers a range of activities including tongues-speech, prediction, encouragement, preaching, teaching, and judgement.

---

48. Barrett, *Acts 1–14,* 602; Peterson, *Acts,* 374. *Did.* 15:1 also associates prophets and teachers, as later did the rabbis—according to rabbinic tradition, the prophets were "the oldest expositors of the Law" (Friedrich and Meyer, "προφήτης," 817). Thus, we should not be surprised to see Luke and the early Christians associate prophets and teachers. If I were to diagram the distinction between prophets and teachers a Venn diagram may best demonstrate the relationship which I am proposing. A part of prophecy includes teaching, and a part of teaching may be prophetic. That said, in practice it would be very difficult to isolate exactly which elements of prophecy and teaching might overlap.

49. Ellis, "The Role of the Christian Prophet in Acts," 56; Brown and Peisker, "Prophet," 87; Peterson, *Acts,* 381.

50. *1 Macc* 4:46; 9:27; 14:41; Josephus, *Contra Ap.* 1.41; Bruce, *Acts,* 275. There is some evidence of this within Luke-Acts in Jesus' allusion to the days of Elijah in Luke 4:25–28.

51. Aune, *Prophecy,* 200; Peterson, *Acts,* 357.

Acts 2:17–21 Within the Subsequent Narrative of Acts

That is not to say that all these terms are synonymous, but rather that "prophecy" has a broad extension in Acts.[52] Therefore, whenever we encounter someone in the narrative speaking by the Spirit we can legitimately term it "prophecy", as we recall the promise of Joel 3:1–5 (LXX) quoted by Peter in Acts 2:17–21.

DREAMS AND VISIONS

As was argued in chapter 1, dreams and visions are closely related to prophecy.[53] The words used for dreams and visions in Acts 2:17 (ἐνυπνίοις and ὁράσεις) do not appear in the narrative again. However, a related word for vision (ὅραμα) appears eleven times.[54]

Koet observes that many of the dreams or visions in Acts command or direct missionary endeavour.[55] Similarly, Johnson considers the "vision" to be a plot device for the calling (and keeping) of key characters to significant tasks.[56] Many of the visions are particular to Paul and concern primarily (though not exclusively) Gentile mission.

An exception to the consistent pattern of "missionary vision" is Stephen's vision (Acts 7:55–56) which sits in a category of its own as the vision of a martyr.[57] His vision serves to vindicate both

---

52. For an explanation of "intension" and "extension" in language see Poythress, *Symphonic Theology*, 55–68.

53. In the OT, dreams and visions are common ways by which God reveals himself and his plans to prophets. Num 12:6; Isa 21:1; Ezek 1:1; Amos 7:1; Oba 1:1; Nah 1:1; Hab 1:1; Zech 1:8.

54. Acts 7:31; 9:10; 9:12; 10:3, 17, 19; 11:5; 12:9; 16:9, 10; 18:9. Dreams or night-visions also occur at 23:11 and 27:23.

55. Koet, "Divine Communication in Luke-Acts," 749. Exceptions to this would be Stephen's vision of the exalted Christ in 7:55, and Paul's "assurance-visions" in 18:9; 23:11 and 27:23.

56. Johnson, *Acts*, 164. For "calling" visions see 9:10; 10:17; 16:9. For "keeping" visions see 18:9; 23:11; 27:23.

57. Witherington, *Acts*, 275; Peterson, *Acts*, 265–67.

THE POWER OF PENTECOST

him as a martyr and Christ as risen Lord and judge.[58] After this point, all of the visions direct key figures in the task of mission.

The first two episodes are recorded in most detail, involve the two key characters, Peter and Paul, and both include double-visions. In 9:3–6 the young man, Saul, has his Damascus road vision of the risen Christ, which appears to be for the purpose of commissioning him to Gentile mission (9:15).[59] Around the same time, Ananias receives a vision from the Lord concerning Saul in 9:10. In 10:3 Cornelius has a vision instructing him to summon Peter, and the next day Peter has his vision of the unclean banquet (10:10–16). The double-visions of Paul and Ananias, and of Peter and Cornelius, demonstrate the unmistakable hand of heavenly guidance.[60] These two episodes, occurring in close proximity to one another, involving key characters, and the double-vision rhetorical device, demonstrate the importance of Gentile mission, and its divine authorization.

Subsequent visions, though briefer, serve to give further specific direction or encouragement to Paul toward the fulfilment of his commission. In 16:9–10 Paul has a night-vision of a man from Macedonia requesting help. From this he concludes that God had called him, along with his companions, to preach the gospel to them also—the result of which, was the establishment of the church at Philippi. In 18:9 Paul has a vision of reassurance, in-

---

58. Bock argues that the standing Son of Man as judge vindicates both Stephen and Christ. *Mart. Ascen, Isa.* 5:9 describes Isaiah as having a vision as he was sawn in two which is probably designed to vindicate him as a true prophet. See Bock, *Acts,* 310–12.

59. Peterson notes this Christophany is both conversion and call. Peterson, *Acts,* 303.

60. See Gen 41:32. Pervo connects the double-visions of Pharaoh (Gen 41:32) to the double-visions of Paul and Ananias, and Peter and Cornelius. *Profit with Delight,* 72–74. See also Bock, *Acts,* 360. Since, in Pharaoh's case the double-vision came to the same person, I think a better case can be made for connecting Pharaoh's double-vision to Peter's three-fold vision in Acts 10.

Acts 2:17–21 Within the Subsequent Narrative of Acts

structing him to continue preaching the gospel in Corinth.[61] In addition there are three further examples of divine communication which may be considered to in the same category as dreams and visions (22:17–21; 23:11; 27:23–24). In Acts 22:17–21 Paul refers back to his time in Jerusalem, probably shortly after his conversion (cf. 9:26–31). Mention of his vision in the temple portrays him as a prophet like Isaiah who also receives a "calling-vision" in the temple (Isa 6:1–10). The temple was also the setting for previous recollections of God's promises concerning the restoration of Israel as a light to the nations (Luke 2:30–32, 38; Acts 3:25).[62] Paul receives further "assurance visions" in 23:11 and 27:23–24 indicating that he must testify before Caesar in Rome. Witherington notes that these subsequent visions (subsequent, that is, to the visions of Acts 9) occur at crisis moments or turning points within the narrative.[63] Further, the wide distribution of visions across the narrative emphasizes heavenly control over the early Christian movement.[64] This aspect of Joel's prophecy is clearly fulfilled in the development of Luke's narrative.

An article by Spencer slightly muddies the waters however.[65] He notes the association of visions with young men in Acts 2:17, and argues that Luke's portrayal of "young men" (νεανίσκοι) is somewhat varied. While we do observe some young men experiencing visions and prophesying in power (like Peter, Paul and Stephen),[66] we also observe the less than inspiring undertakers (Acts 5:10) and the sleepy Eutychus (Acts 20:3). Perhaps this is

---

61. Although Paul's ministry in Corinth included preaching to Jews, the episode follows a familiar pattern of Jewish rejection, and Gentile acceptance (18:6).

62. Witherington, *Acts*, 674; Peterson, *Acts*, 604.

63. Witherington, *Acts*, 693. He cites Acts 9:4; 16:9; 18:9; 22:17; 27:23–24.

64. Barrett, *Acts 15–28*, 771.

65. Spencer, "Wise Up, Young Man," 34–48.

66. Also, let us not forget Paul's nephew who is portrayed in a positive light for informing the authorities of the Jews plans to kill Paul (Acts 23:16–22).

THE POWER OF PENTECOST

Luke's skilful weaving together of the real and the ideal in his portrayal of the life of the early church.

SIGNS AND WONDERS

The phrase "signs and wonders" occurs nine times in Acts, which is significant given that the phrase does not occur at all in Luke, and only once each in Matthew and Mark.[67] The phrase (σημεῖα καὶ τέρατα) is most commonly used in the OT with reference to the events of the exodus[68]—further evidence that Luke is reporting the restoration of Israel in her new exodus.[69] The phrase is almost exclusively used in Acts within Jewish contexts, with the last occurrence being at the Jerusalem council in Acts 15. Perhaps this is evidence that "signs and wonders" are particularly for a Jewish audience, with all the history they evoke.[70]

In Acts, signs and wonders serve a legitimating function. First, they authenticate the key prophetic leader figures—they authenticate Christ (2:22), and serve as prophetic credentials for Christ's servants (2:19, 43; 4:16, 22, 30; 5:12; 6:8; 8:6).[71] In the first summary statement on the life of the early believers we find "many wonders and signs . . . being done through the apostles" (2:43),[72]

---

67. Matt 24:24; Mark 13:22. Rengstorf, "σημεῖον" 229–30. Rengstorf also notes that τέρατα always occurs in combination with σημεῖον.

68. Ex 11:9–10; Dt 6:22; 7:19; 11:3; 28:46; 29:2; Ps 77:43; 134:9; Jer 39:20. In ten out of the fifteen occurrences of the phrase, the referent is the exodus.

69. See Peter's explanation of the healing of the lame man (Acts 3:1–10) in Acts 3:11–26. Peterson, *Acts,* 165.

70. That said, they do appear among Samaritans, and among both Jews and Greeks at the synagogue in Iconium (Acts 14:1–3).

71. Johnson, *Acts,* 108, 146. Peterson, commenting on 2:43, suggests that miracles confirm both the teaching and status of the apostles. He does acknowledge that signs and wonders are not exclusive to the apostles (cf. 6:8; 8:6). Peterson, *Acts,* 162.

72. ESV. Fitzmyer writes, "What revealed the heavenly accreditation of Jesus [2:22] is now used by Luke to confirm the heavenly approbation of the apostles testimony." Fitzmyer, *Acts,* 271. See also Johnson, *Acts,* 58.

which is closely followed by the first detailed report of such an event (3:1–10).[73] A similar summary statement also comes in 5:12, further authenticating the apostles in the face of Jewish opposition. In 6:8 we are introduced to Stephen, a man who was doing "great wonders and signs among the people."[74] Philip is also one who does "signs" which cause the crowds to pay attention to the message (8:6, 13).[75] In the case of Stephen and Philip we may see the necessity of accreditation, particularly as they are not part of the Twelve. Paul is also accredited through signs and wonders. Often noted is the Jesus-Peter-Paul parallelism in the miracles performed.[76] Miracles common to all three include the healing of the lame (Luke 5:17–26; Acts 3:6; 14:10), healing in extraordinary ways (Luke 8:44; Acts 5:15; 19:12), and the raising of the dead (Luke 7:11–17; Acts 9:40; 20:10). Further, Peter and Paul both deliver a judgment sign (Acts 5:5; 13:11). Luke is keen to present both Peter and Paul as being in continuity with Christ.[77] Rengstorf rightly

73. Peter and John's healing of the lame man is considered a "notable sign" in 4:16, 22.

74. ESV. Barrett suggests that Stephen's performance of signs and wonders demonstrates that he is not inferior to the Twelve, rather than showing him to be a model of Christian spirituality (translating "Vorbild des christlichen pneumatikertums")—the view of Roloff, *Die Apostelgeschichte*, 112 cited in Barrett, *Acts 1–14,* 322. In addition, Bock notes the connection between Stephen's character and his miracle working (6:8), a connection seen in respect to vision (Bock, *Acts,* 269–70). Further, as in other instances of signs and wonders, there is a connection with the message (Acts 6:9). Bruce, *Acts,* 186.

75. The signs and wonders are probably intended to authenticate both him and the message, particularly given he is beginning to cross strictly Jewish boundaries.

76. Among others, Neirynck, "The Miracles Stories in the Acts of the Apostles," 205; Fitzmyer, *Acts,* 276; Witherington, *Acts,* 221.

77. Neirynck, "Miracles Stories," 205. This is a key point which Menzies misses when he argues that Luke "consciously distanced the Spirit from direct or exclusive association with miracles" (Menzies, "A Pentecostal Perspective on Signs and Wonders," 269). When we recall the programmatic statement of Jesus in Luke 4:18–19, and see the liberations he performs in the subsequent chapters as *the* Spirit-filled man we can see that it is only by the Spirit that the

states that signs and wonders are "an essential and indispensable part of the divine authentication of the apostles."[78]

Second, signs and wonders, authenticate the message (4:29–30; 14:3).[79] The miracles "draw people into considering the message."[80] O'Reilly describes word and sign as distinct but related "in the closest possible way."[81] The believers pray for God to stretch out his hand,[82] and perform more signs and wonders through Jesus' name as they proclaim the message with boldness (4:29–30).[83] The Samaritan crowds paid close attention to what Philip said when they saw the miraculous signs he performed (8:6). In 14:3 we are told Paul and Barnabas were granted the ability to do signs and wonders by God as he "bore witness to the word of his grace."[84] In almost every occurrence of the miraculous, the word is close at hand.[85] The miracle "becomes a way in which the testimony of

---

followers of Jesus perform the miraculous.

78. Rengstorf, "σημεῖον," 242. Similarly Hardon, "The Miracles Narratives in the Acts of the Apostles" 303–18.

79. Witherington, *Acts,* 203–4.

80. Bock, *Acts,* 326.

81. O'Reilly, *Word and Sign,* 212.

82. Johnson notes that the phrase 'stretch out your hand' further heightens the exodus imagery (Exod 3:20; 6:6; 7:3, 5). Johnson, *Acts,* 85. Also Peterson, *Acts,* 202.

83. Acts 4:30, following immediately on from v. 29, uses the preposition ἐν with the articular infinitive (ἐν τῷ τὴν χεῖρά [σου] ἐκτείνειν) to indicate instrumentality (i.e. "enable your servants to speak your word with great boldness *by means of* the stretching out of your hand to heal and perform miraculous signs and wonders"—my translation). Bruce, *Acts,* 159. BDF §406 notes that ἐν plus the dative articular infinitive conveys the temporal notion of "while" reflecting the Hebrew construction of ב plus infinitive. However, I think Bruce is correct here, in that the temporal does not rule out the instrumental. The temporal (while) could include implied instrumentality.

84. ESV.

85. See Acts 2:42–43; 3:6–12; 4:29–30; 5:12–21; 6:8–10; 8:5–6; 13:6–12; 14:3; 15:7–8, 12; 16:13–18; 19:10–11; 20:7–12. Exceptions occur with the punitive miracle of 5:1–11, the pair of healings performed by Peter (9:32–43) and the snake-bite recovery and healings of Paul on Malta (28:1–10). This point is also made by McCord Adams, "The Role of Miracles in the Structure

the apostles is further borne, the gospel preached, and the Word of God is duly spread."[86]

Third, and related to this, signs and wonders, legitimate the mission. In 15:12 at the Jerusalem council Paul and Barnabas recount the signs and wonders God had done through them among the Gentiles, as evidence for the justification of Gentile mission.[87]

Fourth, it is interesting to consider the geographic, historical, and narratival spread of miracles. Remus notes "Each time the Christian movement is established in a new location, moving from Jerusalem to Judea and Samaria, and "the ends of the earth" (Acts 1:8), miracles are an essential element in the process, so that, finally, all opposition overcome, the reign of God and teaching about Jesus Christ are proclaimed and taught "openly and unhindered" (28:31)."[88] Historically and narratively, Lampe observes the parallelism between Jesus' early miracles (Luke 4:38–40), and Paul's final miracles (Acts 28:8–9). In both cases we are told of many sick people being brought, and healed. The Spirit is thus clearly at work from Jerusalem to the ends of the earth, bearing witness to the new eschatological age.[89]

---

of Luke-Acts," 261–62.

86. Fitzmyer, Acts, 276.

87. Barrett, Acts 15–28, 721–22. Also, Bock, Acts, 502. Fitzmyer agrees, but also sees the signs and wonders as evidence that what Peter has just been saying is true. Fitzmyer, Acts, 549.

88. Remus may be guilty of an over-realized eschatology here in that all opposition is not yet finally overcome (Acts 2:35; 14:22). However, it may be that Remus is employing hyperbole to make his point. Remus, "Miracle," 4:865. Miracles occur in Jerusalem in 2:43; 3:1–10; 5:12–16; 6:8; in Samaria in 8:6–13; in Judea in 9:32–42; and beyond in 14:3, 8–10; 19:11–12; 20:7–12; 28:3–9. Neirynck likewise observes that miracle stories often come at the "beginning of a new period of the Christian mission." Neirynck, "Miracle Stories," 205.

89. Lampe, "Miracles in the Acts of the Apostles," 178. Further, it is interesting to note that Luke refers to the inhabitants of Malta as βάρβαροι (natives—28:4) which heightens the sense of geographical expansion.

THE POWER OF PENTECOST

As in the first exodus, so now in the new, signs and wonders are "instrumental in forming the Israel of the end-time."[90]

SALVATION

An examination of the role of Acts 2:17–21 in the subsequent narrative would be incomplete without consideration of salvation. Salvation is the overarching theme which unifies other elements of the promise.[91] As we observed in chapter 1, the salvation referred to in Joel 3:5 (LXX) is future deliverance from judgment, and thus we find a good number of references in Acts which depict salvation as future deliverance.[92] That said, salvation is not just *from* something, but *for* something, namely physical, social and spiritual restoration, and the presence of the "last days" means that salvation is already inaugurated with its concomitant eschatological *hors d'œuvres*.[93] Evidence that salvation is the overarching theme is seen when we observe the frequency with which prophecy, dreams and visions, or signs and wonders serve the mission of salvation.[94] The Joel quotation indicates that the eschatological time of salvation was to be determined by a particular display of God's power by the Spirit.[95] A special foretaste of new creation restoration (Acts 3:21) is seen, for example, in the physical restoration of the lame man in Acts 3:1–10. Acts 2:17–21 spills over into the subsequent narrative (e.g. 2:42–47; 3:1–10; 4:23–37; 5:12–16) as a present pic-

---

90. O'Reilly, *Word and Sign*, 190.
91. Green, "Salvation to the End of the Earth," 83.
92. Acts 2:21, 40, 47; 11:14; 14:22; 15:1, 11; 16:30, 31.
93. A good example of this can be seen in Acts 2:38–47. Salvation is *from* the curse and consequences of sin, and *for* a community bearing witness to Israel's ongoing restoration.
94. For prophecy and salvation see 2:14–40; 4:8–12; 5:29–32. For dreams and visions and salvation see 9:15; 10:10–16 (cf. 11:14). For signs and wonders and salvation see 2:43; 8:6–13; 14:3, 9; 15:11–12.
95. Joel 3:1–5 (LXX); *4 Ezra* 13; *Test. Levi* 18. Jervell, *Theology of Acts*, 47.

Acts 2:17-21 Within the Subsequent Narrative of Acts

ture of the final salvation that Christ had inaugurated and would consummate at the restoration of all things (3:21).[96]

Salvation for Luke has a broad meaning including, incorporation into the Christ community (2:47), deliverance (27:20-43), healing (4:9, 12), forgiveness of sins (5:31), and Spirit reception (2:38).[97] Indeed the Spirit is the means by which the age of salvation comes as the new Israel fulfil their call to be a light to the nations (Luke. 2:32; Acts 13:47).[98] It is worth noting that the connection between the Spirit, restoration, and physical, social and spiritual salvation fits nicely with the wider context of Joel's prophecy.[99]

CONCLUSION

This chapter has argued that the subsequent narrative charts the fulfilment, not only of Acts 1:8, but also Acts 2:17-21. Tannehill is correct in his assertion that the Joel quotation remains active in the ensuing narrative.[100] As believers receive the promised Spirit, it is evidenced by the various phenomena promised by Joel. They all serve to demonstrate significantly that the restoration of Israel is under way. The various phenomena are not just evidential however—they are also the means by which "Israel" is restored and fulfils her commission to be a light to the nations (cf. 1:8). This can be seen in the close connection between the phenomena described in 2:17-21 and the mission of 1:8. Prophecy, dreams and visions, and

96. I am grateful to Jim Murkett for his insight regarding the relationship between the healing of the lame man in Acts 3:1-10 and Christ's final restoration of all things mentioned in 3:21.

97. Green, "Salvation," 91-95.

98. Witherington, "Salvation and Health in Christian Antiquity," 166.

99. See Joel 3:5-4:21 (LXX).

100. Tannehill, *Narrative Unity,* 32. Here I disagree with the view that the "citations from Joel 3:1-5 (LXX) in Acts 2:17-21 and from Amos 9:11-12 (LXX) in Acts 15:16-17 . . . organize the narrative of Acts and its theological subject matter" (Wall, "Israel and the Gentile Mission," 437-52). This chapter has demonstrated that the fulfilment of the Joel quotation extends beyond Acts 15. Therefore any overly neat division is foreign to Luke's endeavour.

signs and wonders are all connected in various ways to the mission of witness to the ends of the earth.

The difficult question which takes us into the next chapter is, are these events descriptive or prescriptive? To answer that question we need to address Luke's wider purpose in writing. To that we now turn.

4

Acts 2:17–21
Within Luke's Overall Purpose

INTRODUCTION

SO FAR we have argued that Acts 2:17–21 is a programmatic text in the restoration of Israel in her new exodus. In the last chapter we saw the various ways in which the quotation is actively fulfilled in the subsequent narrative, providing evidence that the restoration and new exodus are under way. Having surveyed the numerous examples of prophecy, dreams and visions, and signs and wonders, we turn to consider the role and function of Acts 2:17–21 within Luke's overall purpose in writing. What is Luke intending to convey to his readership? Are there certain perlocutionary effects for which he is aiming?[1] All of this drives at the thorny issue of authorial intent. Before we can examine Luke's overall purpose we need briefly to defend authorial intent as a worthy target to pursue.

The "New Criticism", (which actually began in the early part of the last century) along with structuralist, post-structuralist, deconstructionist, and reader-response models of hermeneutics consider the pursuit of authorial intent to be unimportant and

---

1. Speech-Act Theory is a branch of pragmatic linguistics which considers not just the actual words spoken or written down (locution), but also their intended meaning (illocution) and effect on the hearers/readers (perlocution).

undesirable—worse, an "intentional fallacy."² Important figures within these diverse schools, such as Gadamer, Foucault and Derrida, generally follow the view that speech becomes "alienated" in the act of writing, detached from its author, and therefore its truth must be "stated anew."³ Attempts to discover or take seriously the intent of the author are impossible since, on the one hand it involves speculative psychologising, and on the other hand we bring too much of our own culture, worldview, and presuppositions to discern it properly. In Vanhoozer's terms, the author, once "master of his or her words, has in postmodernity been thoroughly dispossessed."⁴

Therefore, it is suggested, we ought only to focus on what the text says to us as subjects. Of course there is some half-truth here. It is true that we bring our own particular worldview to a text which will, to some degree, influence our interpretation—that is clear and must be acknowledged.⁵ But conceding this does not necessarily exclude the pursuit of authorial intent as a worthy end. It simply cautions us to proceed with care, and exercise appropriate humility acknowledging our own weaknesses. It would be folly on that basis to suppose that authorial intent was not worthy of consideration; real life would be rendered meaningless and not a little difficult.⁶ The law does not permit me to interpret the national

---

2. Of course not all literary critics would deny the possibility of pursuing authorial intent. There is an enormous range of views within these labels. "The Intentional Fallacy" is the title of an article written by Wimsatt and Beardsley in which they argue that "The design or intention of the author is neither available nor desirable as a standard for judging the success of a work of literary art." Wimsatt and Beardsley, "The Intentional Fallacy," 3–18 cited in Thiselton, *Hermeneutics,* 25.

3. Gadamer, *Truth and Method,* 354–56.

4. Vanhoozer, *Is There a Meaning in This Text?* 230.

5. To that end, more moderate reader response theories have much to offer in terms of inviting readers to participate in the narrative filling gaps and joining dots.

6. As Carson says, "The understanding is doubtless never absolutely exhaustive and perfect, but that does not mean the only alternative is to

speed limit sign as "drive as fast as you like." Explaining to the judge that meaning had become detached at the point of writing, and my subjective and experiential interpretation and restating of that meaning led me to the conclusion that I was permitted to drive at one hundred and fifty miles per hour will not excuse me from the penalty of the law. I am expected to understand authorial intent with regard to road signs. Similarly, medics, in prescribing, expect me to understand and respect authorial intent when reading the information that accompanies pharmaceutical products. It would not be sensible to consume an entire box of ibuprofen at the onset of a headache because my interpretation leads me to conclude that two tablets could be interpreted as twenty-four.

Theoretical gymnastics aside let us be serious about listening to authors as they communicate. Let us employ what Osborne has termed the "commonsense argument."[7] Maxwell has done some helpful work bringing the two ideas of authorial intent and reader response together.[8] She posits the idea that the author him or herself has a community readership in mind, whom the author knows, and therefore communicates accordingly. The author is not communicating with entirely anonymous figures. He or she knows the kinds of people they are, the issues they want addressed, the worldview and assumptions they bring, and the way they are likely to approach and understand the text. Similarly, I can project the kind of community this book will be read by. Many (though not all) will be well-educated, Christian, and western. I have an idea of the kinds of frameworks they bring to the text, the questions they will have, their objections and presuppositions. Knowing this I attempt to respect them as I communicate, and expect them to take my intent in communication seriously. This is the only basis for serious and meaningful communication. Without it the

---

dissociate text from speaker, and then locate all meaning in the reader or hearer." *Gagging of God*, 103.

7. Osborne, *Hermeneutical Spiral*, 385.

8. Maxwell, *Hearing Between the Lines*.

notion of communication breaks down, we have no meaningful discourse, and the conversation cannot be taken forward. To quote Vanhoozer, "a text is a communicative action fixed by writing."[9] Therefore, we take communicative intent seriously.

In examining authorial intent there is obviously some caution required to ensure we do not become overly speculative. Sternberg helpfully states, "our only concern is with "embodied" or "objectified" intention . . . communication presupposes a speaker who resorts to certain linguistic and structural tools in order to produce certain affects on the addressee; the discourse accordingly supplies a network of clues to the speaker's intention."[10]

Given the legitimacy of such a project, it is these various tools of literary study that will need to be employed—only then will we be in a position to consider the place of Acts 2:17–21 within Luke's overall purpose.

LUKE'S NARRATIVE STRATEGY IN PURSUING HIS PURPOSE

Gordon Fee has written, concerning the interpretation of narrative, that "historical precedent, to have normative value, must be related to *intent*."[11] Any aspect of Lucan theology, including pneumatology, which is to be embraced as normative must be related to Luke's primary intent in writing, hence a consideration of Luke's overall intent is important at this juncture. It is my contention that Luke is writing to provide Theophilus with certainty concerning the things he had been taught (Luke 1:4).[12] To demonstrate this we

---

9. Vanhoozer, *Is There a Meaning in This Text?* 233.

10. Sternberg, *The Poetics of Biblical Narrative*, 9.

11. Fee, *Gospel and Spirit*, 92. In using the term "normative" I acknowledge that there is a sense in which all scripture has normative value on the reader. I use the term to refer to standards of practice—e.g. in some Pentecostal theology tongues-speech is considered *normative* evidence of Spirit-baptism.

12. For evidence of this see below. It is worth stating here that I believe Luke-Acts to be a unity, therefore see Luke's prologue (Luke 1:1–4) to be

will examine Luke's use of six rhetorical or narratival techniques as his "means of persuasion."[13]

1. Luke's Prologue (Luke 1:1-4)

Darr states that Luke's "ornate opening serves as a powerful rhetorical entrée to the entire work."[14] It follows Greek literary conventions as a preface including a dedication, declaration of subject matter, and statement of reliance on eye-witnesses.[15] Many note that Luke's key self-stated aim, introduced by the *hina* purpose clause at the start of v. 4, is that Theophilus might come to fully know (ἐπιγνῷς) with certainty (ἀσφάλεια, Luke 1:4) the things he had been taught.[16] Further, Fitzmyer suggests that positioning the noun, ἀσφάλειαν, at the end of the sentence is for emphasis.[17] Certain assurance for Theophilus of things seen and heard is perhaps the primary, though not exclusive, aim for Luke. Luke's self-characterisation of his work is also important. He describes his work as a close investigation (παρηκολουθηκότι—v. 3), involving careful ordering (ἀκριβῶς καθεξῆς—v. 3), and eyewitness sources

---

a prologue to his entire two-volume work. See the arguments put forward for the unity of Luke-Acts in Verheyden, "The Unity of Luke-Acts," *contra* Walters, *Assumed Authorial Unity of Luke and Acts*.

13. Aristotle defined rhetoric as the "ability, in each case, to see the available means of persuasion." Aristotle, *Rh.* 1.2.1. In examining Lucan intent by considering rhetorical strategies present within the narrative we are not speculatively psychologising regarding Luke's intent—it is encoded within the narrative.

14. Darr, *On Character Building*, 54.

15. Bauckham, *Jesus and the Eyewitnesses*, 116–24.

16. Maddox, *The Purpose of Luke-Acts*, 183–86; Shepherd, *Narrative Function*, 112–13; Yamada, "A Rhetorical History: The Literary Genre of the Acts of the Apostles," 244. For ἐπιγνῷς carrying the intentional sense of "fully know" or "realise" see Bultmann, "ἐπιγινώσκω" *TDNT* 1:704; Hackenberg, "ἐπιγινώσκω" *EDNT* 2:24. Schmidt defines ἀσφάλεια as a "certain, solid, or reliable knowledge." Schmidt, "ἀσφάλεια," *TDNT* 1:506.

17. Fitzmyer, *Luke I–IX*, 300. See also Reiling and Swellengrebel, *A Translator's Handbook on the Gospel of Luke*, 13.

(αὐτόπται—v. 2), all serving to give credence to Luke's endeavour.[18] Fitzmyer argues that the verb, κατηχήθης (v. 4), conveys the sense of "instruct" or "teach" and therefore, Luke's two-volume work is an attempt to give further instruction and assurance to an interested enquirer, if not a catechumen or neophyte.[19] Given Luke's emphases, displayed in plot and pace, he is conveying "certainty" regarding the message of salvation and legitimation of Gentile mission.[20] Observe, for example, the consistent references throughout Acts to God's hand being upon the new community and the word continuing spread,[21] or the consistent emphasis on the legal innocence of this new sect,[22] and one certainly gains the impression that Luke is providing an "apology" for Christianity—an apology that would be necessary in the face of Jewish revolt. As Johnson observes, "the success of the Gentile mission and the failure of the Jewish mission raised an issue of theodicy . . . how could Gentiles have confidence in their faith? Could God abandon

---

18. Johnson, *Luke,* 28. Further, there is a strong possibility that what was "entrusted" to Luke was in written form—a written source from the eyewitnesses. Cadbury makes a strong case for taking the αὐτόπται and ὑπηρέται together, hence what we have here is apostolic testimony, possibly written down. See Cadbury, "Commentary on the Preface of Luke," 497–500.

19. Fitzmyer, *Luke I-IX,* 289–301. As Johnson points out, the work was probably intended for wider circulation as well, giving instruction and assurance to Gentiles that God had been faithful to his own word of promise to both Israel and the Gentiles. Johnson, *Luke,* 9–10.

20. We do not have space here to conduct a thorough examination of Lucan emphases revealed through plot and pace. For a concise summary see Maddox, *The Purpose of Luke-Acts,* 180–87. See also Fitzmyer, *Luke I-IX,* 9; Bock, *Luke 1:1–9:50,* 14. Dillon notes that the same word (ἀσφάλεια) is used at the conclusion of Peter's Pentecost speech (Acts 2:36) and suggests that the ἀσφάλεια referred to in the prologue refers to the same thing—namely that God has made Jesus both Lord and Christ. Dillon, "Previewing Luke's Project from his Prologue," 226. The only other occurrences of ἀσφάλεια in Acts are in 5:23 and 16:23 which both refer to the security (ἀσφάλεια) of imprisonment.

21. Acts 2:47; 6:7; 9:31; 12:24; 16:5.

22. Acts 16:36; 18:15; 25:20; 26:31–32.

them as well?"²³ Therefore, Luke shows how "the Gentile Church of his own day emerged in continuity from a faithful and restored Israel."²⁴

2. Prophecy and Fulfilment

Prophecy and fulfilment, in terms of salvation history, is a particularly Lucan emphasis.²⁵ The fulfilment of Scripture, and the necessity of such fulfilment, is frequently expressed by the impersonal verb δεῖ (it is necessary) occurring twenty-eight times in Luke-Acts.²⁶ That is significantly more than either Matthew or Mark, and Cosgrove has argued it is used to demonstrate the necessity of fulfilment of the divine plan as well as providing divine mandates to be obeyed.²⁷ It is a powerful rhetorical device to authenticate the account.²⁸ In addition there are many other prophetic predictions within Luke-Acts. Rothschild argues there are basically two kinds of prophetic prediction observed—the human, and the divine. She further divides divine prediction into i) predictions from heavenly messengers; ii) predictions from the risen Christ; iii) predictions from the Holy Spirit.²⁹ Heavenly messengers predict the birth of John the Baptist (Luke 1:13–17; fulfilled in Luke 1:57–66), and the birth of Jesus (Luke 1:26–37; fulfilled in Luke 2:7). The risen Christ foretells the reception of the Spirit by the disciples (Acts 1:8; fulfilled in Acts 2:1–13), and the sufferings of Paul (Acts 9:16; fulfilled

23. Johnson, *Luke*, 30.
24. Ibid.
25. Fitzmyer, *Luke I–IX*, 180.
26. Luke 2:49; 4:43; 9:22; 13:33; 17:25; 19:5; 21:9; 22:37; 24:7,26,44; Acts 1:16,21; 3:21; 4:12; 5:29; 9:6,16; 14:22; 15:5; 16:30; 17:3; 19:21; 20:35; 23:11; 24:19; 25:10; 27:24. Compare this to only four occurrences in Mark (8:31; 13:7,10,14) and three in Matthew (16:21; 24:6; 26:54). Fitzmyer, *Luke I–IX*, 180.
27. Cosgrove, "The Divine ΔΕΙ in Luke-Acts," 174.
28. Rothschild, *Luke-Acts and the Rhetoric of History*, 185–212.
29. Ibid., 176. I would include predictions made by Christ in the gospel as well here (eg. about his death—Luke 9:22, 44; 18:31–33).

in Acts 9:23). The Holy Spirit is the one who speaks through the OT prophecies (e.g. Acts 1:16; 4:25; 28:25) as well as predicting the famine (Acts 11:28) and imprisonment (Acts 21:11; fulfilled in Acts 21:30).

Human prophetic predictions occur through Zechariah (Luke 1:76; fulfilled in Luke 3:1–20), Paul (Acts 13:11), and Agabus (Acts 11:28). In addition the number of OT prophecies cited as fulfilled demonstrates the continuity of Luke-Acts with the OT story demonstrating that God's plan has not failed, but is rather finding its fulfilment. Peterson concludes that at one level prophecy and fulfilment functions as a legitimation device.[30] Rothschild goes further arguing that the purpose of this rhetorical device is to "sanction the author's version of the events" and is a "subtle form of persuasion."[31] The fulfilment of Joel's prophecy occurs not only on the day of Pentecost, but also in the subsequent narrative, giving strong evidence for the veracity of Luke's account.

3. Repetition

Several scholars observe Luke's fondness for repetition, or what has been termed "informational redundancy."[32] Pervo argues that repetition serves to highlight particularly important or significant events for the author.[33] Such repetitions can be seen in recounting the conversion of Paul (Acts 9; 22; 26) and Cornelius (Acts 10; 11; 15), the call to Gentile mission (Acts 13:46; 18:6; 28:28), and prison rescues (Acts 5:19–20; 12:6–12; 16:25–40). Luke's

---

30. Peterson, "The Motif of Fulfilment and the Purpose of Luke-Acts," 103.

31. Rothschild, *Luke-Acts,* 180, 183.

32. For the term "informational redundancy" see Sternberg, *The Poetics of Biblical Narrative,* 476–81. For its use in Acts see Witherup, who uses the term "functional redundancy." Witherup, "Functional Redundancy in the Acts of the Apostles," 67–86; Witherup, "Cornelius Over and Over and Over Again," 45–66. See also Pervo, *The Mystery of Acts,* 57–65.

33. Pervo, *Mystery,* 57. Osborne too lists repetition as a narratival tool used for emphasis. Osborne, *The Hermeneutical Spiral,* 162.

"threepeats"[34] serve the function of assurance in terms of both the importance of a theme and the veracity of his narrative. In respect to Acts 2:17–21, chapter 3 argued that we do see repeated instances of the phenomena mentioned demonstrating to the audience that the Christ who poured out the Spirit is continuing to work (Acts 1:1). This raises further questions in considering particular functions of such phenomena. For example, is Luke's intent in repeatedly portraying tongues-speech to legitimate controversial people groups or give a paradigm of conversion experience? Similarly, is the repetition of "signs and wonders" intended as verification of the new exodus, or a pattern for *normal* Christian experience? Contextual factors and a close reading of the text must dictate, but it is important to see that repetition is far from clumsy editing of sources; it serves to give clarity, emphasis, and assurance as to the key themes and reliability of what would have been a primarily aural work.[35] In the context of Luke's overall purpose it seems that repetition of the miraculous phenomena serves to highlight the ongoing work of Christ through the Spirit. Luke is more concerned with persuading the reader that all he has said about Christ is true, rather than providing the church with a manual to regulate their gatherings.

4. Recurrence/Mimesis

Many have noted how Luke's portrayal of Jesus is often patterned on significant OT figures.[36] For example, the account of Jesus raising to life the son of the widow in Nain (Luke 7:11–17) recalls Elijah's miracle in 1 Kings 17.[37] Jesus' miraculous provision of bread in the wilderness (Luke 9:10–17) "attested Jesus' affinity

---

34. For the term "threepeats" see Pervo, *Mystery,* 57.
35. See Witherup, "Cornelius," 64–66; Rothschild, *Luke-Acts,* 138–39; Haenchen, *The Acts of the Apostles,* 357.
36. This of course is not unique to Luke.
37. Fitzmyer, *Luke I–IX,* 656; Pervo, *Mystery,* 86.

with the hoped-for prophet-like-Moses" (cf. Acts 3:22; 7:37).[38] Luke's infancy narrative portrays Jesus as the Davidic King (Luke 1:32–33; 2:4), a theme picked up in the speeches of Acts (2:22–41; 13:16–41; 15:13–21).[39] In turn, Peter and Paul perform miracles reminiscent of Jesus', putting them in clear association with their risen and exalted master. Like Jesus, both Peter and Paul heal lame men (Luke 5:17–26; Acts 3:1–10; 14:8–10), raise the dead (Luke 7:11–17; Acts 9:36–43; 20:7–12), and heal in extraordinary ways (Luke 8:44; Acts 5:15–16; 19:12).[40] Pervo claims that the rhetorical effect of such mimesis is to lend authority and trustworthiness to the account.[41] As Paul would say, "it was not done in a corner" (Acts 26:26). Such signs and wonders authenticate the Messiah, his messengers, and their message fulfilling a similar role to the signs and wonders of the first exodus.

This mimesis is not limited to the Jewish scriptures however. The last two chapters particularly play on themes, stories and heroes from ancient Greek literature. The theme in Acts 27–28 of the key character who takes a sea voyage, is assailed by storms, yet vindicated by God possesses obvious parallels to those familiar with the works of Homer and Virgil.[42] Luke is adroit at using the types and conventions of his time to persuade the readers of the trustworthiness of his account and the divine hand upon Jesus and his followers.

---

38. Turner, *Power,* 239.

39. For an outline, explanation, and defence of Jesus' Davidic Kingship see Strauss, *Davidic-Messiah,* 87–193.

40. See McCord Adams, "Role of Miracles," 260–61. Puskas also notes various parallels between Paul and Jesus in the trial accounts. Puskas, *The Conclusion of Luke-Acts*, 67–70.

41. Pervo, *Mystery,* 84. See also Rothschild, *Luke-Acts,* 129.

42. Virgil, *Aeneid* 1:50–255; Homer, *Od.* 5:290–470; 9:61–81; 12:201–303. For more on this theme in Acts 27–28 see Miles and Trompf, "Luke and Antiphon," 259–67.

5. Eyewitnesses[43]

The fifth feature of Lucan rhetoric we will observe is his tendency toward, in Rothschild's terms, hyperbole.[44] This is seen most clearly in Luke's amplification of eyewitnesses.[45] Luke claims to be working from eyewitness (αὐτόπται) testimony in Luke 1:2. Although this is the only occurrence of this word, Luke employs another noun, μάρτυς (witness), fifteen times.[46] Compare this to Matthew (twice—18:16; 26:25) and Mark (once—14:63) and we can see a Lucan emphasis.[47] It is significant that five times in Acts Peter claims the disciples were witnesses of Jesus' life, death, and resurrection (2:32; 3:15; 5:32; 10:39, 41)—a further example of repetition emphasizing reliability. Also significant is Paul's acknowledgment of the special importance of Jesus' first disciples as witnesses (13:31). He himself is included as a witness of things seen and heard in 22:15 and 26:16. Luke's reliable witnesses stand in stark contrast to the false witnesses seen persecuting Jesus' followers (6:13; 25:7). The oft-discussed "we-passages" in Acts (Acts 16:10–17; 20:5–15; 21:1–18; 27:1–28:16) offer further eyewitness authentication to the account.[48] The use of "witness" language, and the witness of the αὐτόπται and μάρτυρες, as well as the Holy Spirit

---

43. This subtitle along with the next is taken from the title of one of Clare Rothschild's chapters entitled "Eyewitnesses and Epitomizing as Historical Rhetoric" in Rothschild, *Luke-Acts,* 213–289.

44. Rothschild, *Luke-Acts,* 213. The use of the term "hyperbole" is not meant to imply that Luke is being less than honest. It is rather a rhetorical technique designed to create an impression—i.e. "every nation under heaven" (Acts 2:5).

45. Ibid., 214–18.

46. Luke 11:48; 24:48; Acts 1:8, 22; 2:32; 3:15; 5:32; 6:13; 7:58; 10:39, 41; 13:31; 22:15; 26:16, 20.

47. Denaux and Corstjens, *The Vocabulary of Luke,* 388.

48. Hengel, *Acts and the History of Earliest Christianity,* 66; Witherington, *Acts,* 480–86

(5:32), more than satisfies the legal requirement of Deut 19:15, and provides excellent evidence for the veracity of Luke's testimony.[49]

6. Epitomization

The final rhetorical tool we shall observe is the other aspect to Luke's "hyperbole"—that is his epitomization of the early Christian community. Summary statements or passages can be found in Acts 2:42–47; 4:32–34; 5:12–16; 6:7; 9:31; 12:24; 16:5; 19:20. These summaries serve not only to advance the plot-line, but also to give Luke's readers assurance of God's hand of blessing upon the early Christian community.[50] The success of this movement along with the portrayal of their unity demonstrates the Lordship of Christ, as the only one who can bring success and true unity.[51] Luke uses the idea of unity versus disunity to demonstrate the divine power at work amongst the Christian community in the face of opposition and persecution. The community forming power of the Holy Spirit adds further authentication to the risen Christ's new community, and ultimately to the risen Christ himself.[52] Such positive characterization is one of the methods Luke employs to persuade the reader/hearer to join the story and become a part of this community. That also might explain the abrupt ending to his second volume. He is inviting the auditor to become his third volume. It is interesting to observe that part of this epitomization in two instances includes signs and wonders (Acts 2:43; 5:12). Again,

49. Trites shows how the juridical theme of "witness" is used by Luke to lend credibility to his account. See Trites, *The New Testament Concept of Witness,* 128–53.

50. Sheeley, *Narrative Asides in Luke-Acts,* 137–76.

51. Thompson, *One Lord, One People,* 57–104.

52. Ibid,. 135–70; Wenk, *Community-Forming Power,* 268–70. Thompson states, "Luke highlights the unity of those who come under the reign of Jesus the Christ . . . Those in turmoil and disorder, however, are explicitly said to be in the realm of Caesar's reign" (148–49). For examples of the unity of the Christian community opposed to the disunity of opposition see Acts 2:46; 4:32; 6:5; 14:4; 17:8.;19:29–32; 23:7; 28:25.

Acts 2:17–21 Within Luke's Overall Purpose

this draws us back to the question of whether Luke's intent is to provide a paradigm of church practice in every time and place, or whether Luke's intent is divine verification of this group of people.[53] It seems the latter is more appropriate to Luke's overarching purpose. For the reader or auditor the summary statements have a powerful rhetorical effect.

Summary

In summary, all of these rhetorical devices—the prologue, prophecy and fulfilment, repetition, mimesis, eyewitnesses, and epitomization—are all utilised together to bring ἀσφάλεια (certainty—Luke 1:4) to Luke's audience. That, it has been argued, is Luke's primary intent in crafting his narrative. In the words of Darr, it is a text "designed to persuade its readers to become believing witnesses."[54] Luke is himself following the apostles in trying to communicate effectively and persuasively (Acts 14:1). As we move toward considering what role Acts 2:17–21 plays in this, we must now consider what role the Holy Spirit more generally plays in Luke's endeavour.

---

53. The verification may be of divine blessing on the Christian community in general, or verification of the apostles as the Lord's appointed witnesses. In some ways it need not be an either-or situation. The portrayal of the community is an indication of God's favour upon, and work among, them. In as much as they display the evidence of the Lord Jesus' rule over them, and the Spirit's work among them, they serve as a model community. The fruit of the Spirit's work will be different for communities in different times and places. For example, we consider the meeting in the temple courts and sharing of all possessions to be situational. Why not also signs and wonders? Signs and wonders may serve Luke's intention of presenting the early Christian community as a "new Israel" in a new exodus. However subsequent communities' experience will also include fruit of the Spirit's work—it is just the specific expression which may differ. This is where Fee's distinction between norm and pattern is helpful. We may observe the pattern and discern the norm to reach the circumstantial application.

54. Darr, *On Character Building*, 53.

THE POWER OF PENTECOST

THE ROLE OF THE HOLY SPIRIT IN LUKE'S PROJECT

We have argued that Luke's aim is to bring assurance to his readers. This aim is achieved by means of various rhetorical strategies already observed within his two-fold work. We would therefore expect Luke's presentation of the Holy Spirit to be consistent with his express aims. After we have considered the role of the Holy Spirit in Luke's project more widely, we will be in a better position to evaluate the purpose of Acts 2:17–21.

Two significant studies, by Hur and Shepherd, have both observed the Spirit's narrative function in contributing toward narrative reliability.[55] Shepherd argues that the Holy Spirit plays a "crucial function in Luke's quest to give assurance to his readers."[56] Luke achieves this in a variety of ways. The Spirit speaks, fills, acts, and empowers in the development of the plot. He is characterised positively, sometimes in explicit contrast to Satanic powers (e.g. Luke 4:1–14; Acts 13:6–12). A brief overview of the Spirit's function in Luke-Acts will serve to demonstrate this.

There is a concentration of references to the Spirit at the beginning of both Luke's first and second volumes. In the infancy narratives (Luke 1–2), we learn in Luke 1:15 that John will be filled with the Holy Spirit. Elizabeth too is filled (1:41) as is John's father, Zechariah, who prophesies his son's future ministry (1:67–80). It is the Spirit who "overshadows" Mary enabling her to conceive (1:35) and bear witness to the plan of God in her *Magnificat* (1:46–55). Simeon is described as being under the influence of the Spirit three times in 2:25–27, and though not explicit, it may be that Anna, the elderly prophetess, likewise possessed the Spirit of prophecy. In these first chapters the Spirit is portrayed as empowering people to witness to God's plan of salvation in Jesus. The Spirit's presence, inspiring the human characters, assures the reader of the reliabil-

---

55. Shepherd, *Narrative Function*; Hur, *Dynamic Reading*.
56. Shepherd, *Narrative Function*, 112.

ity of what these characters proclaim, and thus, the reliability of Luke's narrative.[57]

The beginning of Jesus' ministry sees the double attestation of the Spirit and the Father at his baptism (3:22), closely followed by his temptation, where he is also said to be "full of the Holy Spirit" (4:1). After his temptation Jesus returns "in the power of the Spirit" (4:14) and the opening of Jesus' programmatic sermon in the synagogue begins with the words "The Spirit of the Lord is upon me" (Luke 4:18–19).[58] Luke wants his readers to be in no doubt that Jesus is *the* Spirit-filled man, and as such is considered utterly reliable within the narrative.

Having established the narrative reliability of the main character, Jesus, there are only a handful of other references to the Holy Spirit in the rest of Luke's gospel. The Spirit inspires Jesus' prayer in 10:21, and the other occurrences refer to the future ministry of the disciples (11:13; 12:12; 24:36–53). By the end of the gospel the Spirit is characterized as the "source of inspired witness" and the stage is set for his continued work through Jesus' followers in Acts.[59] It is clear then, that the Holy Spirit is a key character in Luke's narrative, bringing narrative reliability, even before we get to Acts 2.

The beginning of Acts picks up where Luke's first volume left off—both mention the Spirit (Luke 24:49; Acts 1:4–5, 8), and it is worth noting the Spirit again appears in the key programmatic texts (Acts 1:8; 2:17–21; cf. Luke 4:18–19). Again, key characters are said to be filled with the Holy Spirit;[60] the Spirit is a witness to the gospel (Acts 5:32); and key groups are verified.[61] At each new frontier (geographical and sociological) the Spirit provides

57. Ibid., 124.

58. Luke 4:18, ESV. See also Peter's retrospective summary in Acts 10:37–38.

59. Shepherd, *Narrative Function*, 150.

60. Acts 2:4; 4:8, 31; 6:5; 7:55; 11:24; 13:9.

61. Acts 8:14–17; 10:44–48; 11:14–18; 15:8; 19:1–7. Hur, *Dynamic Reading*, 230.

"certainty" of the divine hand at work acting as God's "mission director."[62] Bonnah states "The Holy Spirit directs, determines and legitimates almost all that the narrator writes about in the Acts of the Apostles."[63] As the reader observes the divine hand, by means of the Spirit, authenticating messengers, message, and mission, he can have ἀσφάλεια regarding the things heard (Luke 1:4).[64] It is an emotive and vivifying participative experience.

Thus, the Holy Spirit as a character brings assurance or certainty of the things taught by Luke. As in John's Gospel, he (the Spirit) points away from himself and testifies to Jesus as exalted Son, and his project of kingdom restoration.[65] Therefore to claim any one aspect of his work as paradigmatic misses the point of Luke's (and the Spirit's) work. His ministry in whatever he does is "to point people to Jesus as the crucified, risen, and exalted Lord"[66] bringing the long awaited restoration of Israel (Luke 2:25) and inaugurating the times of refreshing (Acts 3:19). Let us now return to where we started, with Acts 2:17–21.

ACTS 2:17–21 IN LUKE'S OVERALL PURPOSE

When the Spirit falls on the day of Pentecost in fulfilment of Joel 3:1–5 (LXX) what we have is not an intended paradigm for conversion, but rather tangible evidence, witnessed by more than three thousand that Jesus is the risen and exalted Davidic Messiah, sat at the right hand of God the Father, pouring out what had just been seen and heard. All of the OT promises concerning the new covenant are brought to fruition and the last days are inaugurated. Acts 2 is about the climax of Israel's story as she is empowered to be the light to the nations as always intended. It is a key turn-

---

62. Hur, *Dynamic Reading*, 266.
63. Bonnah, *The Holy Spirit*, 265.
64. Shepherd, *Narrative Function*, 219.
65. John 16:12–14; Acts 5:32; 7:55; 16:7.
66. Schreiner, *New Testament Theology*, 450.

ing point in redemptive history, and the visible fulfilment of Joel 3:1–5 (LXX) is the evidence of what Luke has presented in his gospel—this Jesus is both Lord and Christ. The tongues of fire and the xenolalia are the sensory aids pointing to this truth. The Holy Spirit in Luke is certainly about empowering for witness, but more than that, in Luke's purpose the Holy Spirit empowers for sure and certain witness to the fact that God has made this Jesus both Christ and Lord. In the context of Acts 1–2, the rest of Acts, and Luke's wider project, the primary purpose of Acts 2:17–21 is to tell us as much about who Jesus is, than who is followers are to be.

This is, of course, not to say that Acts 2:17–21 has nothing to say regards contemporary charismatic praxis, and it is indeed time to tackle the looming elephant in the room. What is the relationship between the Spirit-wrought phenomena in Acts and the role of the Holy Spirit in the contemporary church? We are now a little closer to formulating an answer to that question.

5

Acts 2:17–21 in Contemporary Debate

INTRODUCTION

WHAT THEN of Acts 2:17–21? Is it a paradigm for contemporary ecclesiological or missional praxis, or a unique unrepeatable event in salvation history?

As mentioned in the introduction, Acts 2 is a *crux interpretum* in the debate, with proponents of differing viewpoints relying heavily on the Pentecost pericope.[1] MacArthur is worth citing again: "without question, the second chapter of Acts is *the key passage* of Scripture from which Pentecostals and charismatics develop their theology."[2] Therefore, how one views contemporary application will depend on how one understands the promise of Pentecost.

SURVEYING THE SCENE

On one side of the debate, there are a large number of scholars who argue that since Pentecost is a redemptively climactic and unique moment, the events associated with it are also unique and unrepeatable in subsequent generations of the church. MacArthur, for example, argues that "the event recorded in Acts was a unique

---

1. For example, Menzies' article, previously cited is entitled "Acts 2:17–21." Similarly, arguing for a cessationist position, Richard Gaffin's book is entitled "*Perspectives on Pentecost.*"

2. MacArthur, *Charismatic Chaos*, 212. Emphasis mine.

wonder. This was the first and last Pentecost for the church."³ Stott, sees the fulfilment of the OT promise as a dramatic picture of what was finally to come, and thus not normative.⁴ Likewise, Gaffin sees Pentecost as primarily redemptive-historical and therefore Acts 2 does not establish a pattern—"the history that interests Luke is *finished*."⁵ These authors are correct in asserting that Pentecost is a climactic moment in redemptive history, and that its evidential and constitutive significance are primary for Luke, but they do not deal adequately with the social and temporal delimitation of the promise. The promise is for *all* God's people (2:17, 18, 38), and it covers the entire period of "the last days". Ferguson attempts to offer a middle-way which is potentially helpful. He distinguishes between the "redemptive-historical" once-for-all events and the "personal-existential" ongoing effects. This is a helpful distinction providing a profitable avenue of exploration. The difficulty is determining which events or phenomena fall into which category. For example, are signs and wonders part of the initial event or ongoing experience? Ferguson offers little advice on how to address that question and presents what is essentially a cessationist position, open to the possibility of providential miracles.⁶

On the other side of the debate, there are many who argue that Pentecost does give a paradigm for the church in every place and age. Deere observes that the phenomenon mentioned in Acts 2:17–21 make an appearance in every chapter of Acts (except chapter 17) and thus represent *normal* Christianity.⁷ Michael Green argues that what began at Pentecost "has not ended. Nor

---

3. MacArthur, *Charismatic Chaos*, 217. Similarly Robertson argues that "all revelatory signs and wonders have stopped" and "all those former ways of God's making his will known to his church have now ceased." Robertson, *The Final Word*, 58, 60.

4. Stott, *Baptism and Fullness*, 28–30.

5. Gaffin. "Cessationist," 38. Emphasis original. See also Gaffin, *Perspectives*, 14–22.

6. Ferguson, *Holy Spirit*, 79–92; 207–39.

7. Deere, *Surprised By The Voice of God*, 60–63.

will it end until the completion of God's purposes for this world at the return of Christ."[8] Douglas Oss notes the use of "the last days" (Acts 2:17) and says there is no evidence that those days are divided or changed prior to the *parousia*,[9] and Ruthven, commenting on Acts 2, notes that "Acts promises the Pentecostal Spirit of power and prophecy to the full extent of both geographical and temporal limits, contradicting cessationism."[10] This view rightly highlights that the democratization of the Spirit is without temporal, social, or geographical limits. However, it fails to satisfactorily outline the ways in which Pentecost (and its associated events and people) are unique or special within redemptive history. Neither, it would seem, are these authors entirely consistent in their approach. There are not, for example, many calling for more Spirit encounters like those experienced by Ananias and Sapphira (Acts 5). There is a danger, on both sides of the debates, in picking and choosing those elements considered normative.

A THIRD WAY?

There is another way to address the question—a way which has been little considered in the ongoing debates.[11] Part of the problem, on both sides, in attempting to construct a Lucan pneumatology, is a failure to read the narrative *as* narrative. Too many, whether it be in the areas of ecclesiological polity, sacramentology, or pneumatology, approach the narrative looking for proof texts to support their position, with little consideration for narratival authorial intent.[12] I propose to address the question by considering

---

8. Green, *I Believe in the Holy Spirit*, 16.

9. Oss, "Pentecostal/Charismatic," 267.

10. Ruthven, *On the Cessation of the Charismata*, 125. For others who share a similar opinion regarding the normative aspect of Acts see Keener, *Gift and Giver*, 95; Twelftree, *People of the Spirit*, 208.

11. A couple of exceptions would be Hur, *Dynamic Reading* and Shepherd, *Narrative Function*.

12. Gaventa states "any attempt to do justice to the theology of Acts must

Acts 2:17-21 in Contemporary Debate

Luke's narrative *as* narrative—that is to consider Luke's intent in presenting his narrative.

Let us recall the insights already gathered in chapter 4. We have already seen that Luke's purpose in writing is to provide Theophilus with "certainty" concerning the things taught. Those things included teaching about God's plan of salvation revealed in Christ. The purpose of such assurance, we argued in chapter 4, was to provide a theodicy regarding Israel's place in God's purposes. Luke demonstrates the continuity of God's purposes by outlining his material in terms of the restoration of Israel. The Spirit as a character provides narrative reliability to Luke's claims by inspiring and empowering key characters. When the narrative arrives at Pentecost, the pouring out of the Spirit fulfils the promise of Joel (and the Father), and demonstrates the divine hand which rests upon this early Jesus-following movement. It is a climactic moment in Luke's story as the pouring out of the Spirit (and his observable activity) testifies to the reality of the exaltation of Christ and the inauguration of "the last days." As readers (or auditors) we are given compelling evidence by the Spirit that the Davidic King as ascended to his throne and is now ruling every nation under heaven. As the narrative progresses, the Spirit provides further evidence of this (seen in prophecies, signs and wonders, and dreams and visions), which further bolsters Luke's claim to reliability.

To return to the question that opened this chapter, does Luke intend us to construct norms for how the Spirit will work in our churches today? The answer is not a straightforward "yes" or "no." On the one hand we can say that it is not Luke's primary intent to provide successive generations of churches with a blueprint for gatherings or mission. Rather, Luke intends the reader, through his various rhetorical techniques (including his presentation of the Spirit), to know with certainty that the coming of the Spirit demonstrates that God has made Jesus both Lord and Christ (Acts

---

struggle to reclaim the character of Acts as a narrative." Gaventa, "Toward A Theology of Acts," 150.

2:36)—the Spirit's empowering and verifying work bears witness to the Lordship of Christ. Everything in Acts 2 moves toward the climax of vv. 36–40. But, on the other hand, patterns like those relayed by Luke are inevitably, to some degree, formative. Communities cannot help but be shaped by the texts which form them, and it would be surprising if early Christian communities had no expectation whatsoever of enjoying the same dynamic Spirit empowered existence as those to whom they are joined in Christ by the Spirit.

I return to Fee's helpful chapter in his book on hermeneutics. He makes the useful distinction between norms and patterns.[13] He notes that while we may not have norms (in the strict sense of the word) regarding charismatic praxis, we do have observable patterns that may or may not be repeatable in the church in subsequent generations. He states, "what is *incidental* to the primary intent of the narrative may indeed reflect an author's theology . . . but it cannot have the same didactic value as what the narrative was *intended* to teach."[14] This insight is helpful to proponents on all sides; it guards against the extremes of dismissing or prescribing what is incidental to primary intent. For example, observing the Spirit-wrought miracles performed at the frontiers of mission (Acts 8:5–6) does not present us with a *norm* for contemporary pioneering missionary work—that is not Luke's intent.[15] Luke's

---

13. Fee, *Gospel and Spirit*, 95–103. William Menzies, responding to Fee's work turns the question around asking whether you can demonstrate that Luke did *not* intend to depict his description of early church practice as normative. He goes on to accuse Fee or arbitrariness in what he would consider normative. However, it seems that Menzies proposal is equally guilty of the charge but has even fewer constraints than Fee's. See Menzies, "The Methodology of Pentecostal Theology," 1–15.

14. Fee, *Gospel and Spirit*, 92. Emphasis original.

15. In that sense there is a geography of signs and wonders. The signs and wonders which Jerusalem have experienced now occur even among Samaritans (Acts 8:5–6) and Gentiles (Acts 14:3). This is appealed to by Paul in Acts 15:12 as legitimation for Gentile mission. See Sleeman, *Geography and the Ascension Narrative*, 177.

Acts 2:17–21 in Contemporary Debate

intent is to demonstrate that God's salvation extends *even* unto Samaritans. But neither can we dismiss contemporary accounts of the miraculous on the basis that such miraculous events are incidental to didactic intent. There is a pattern which does repeat (Acts 14:8–10; 20:9–10; 28:1–10). It does not repeat in every place and location, but does recur at certain points. Consequently, we have a pattern which may or may not be repeatable today, but that is different from making it a *norm*. Blanket dismissal or prescription of such phenomena today, based on Luke's narrative alone, is a misappropriation, based on a misunderstanding of narrative function. With narrative-theological antennae up, we may now consider some tentative proposals regarding contemporary pneumatology.

THOUGHTS ON CONTEMPORARY PRACTICE

Four particular phenomena from Acts (particularly Acts 2) merit consideration. These are: tongues-speech, dreams and visions, signs and wonders, and prophecy. We shall consider each in turn.

Tongues-Speech

As observed in chapter 3, there are three occurrences of tongues-speech in Acts (2:4; 10:46; 19:6). The only missional use of tongues-speech occurs in Acts 2, and there, the primary function of the gift is to attest Christ as exalted Messiah, and the disciples as his authoritative servants.[16] Tongues-speech serves to legitimate early Gentile believers in Acts 10 (and possibly Acts 8), and John's

---

16. Interestingly there are citations of people being miraculously given a gift of a certain language for the sake of missionary endeavour. Peter Wagner cites a case he knows first-hand of a missionary couple in Argentina being given miraculously the gift of Spanish. I have no reason to doubt Wagner's claim—he himself acknowledges this to be the only case he personally knows, and that in 99.9% of cases missionaries have to spend years learning languages. That God could perform such a miracle I have no reason to doubt; whether it is the gift of tongues as seen in Acts or something analogous I confess uncertainty. See Wagner, *The Third Wave*, 102–05.

historically liminal disciples in Acts 19. The didactic function of this pattern of tongues-speech is the evidential attestation of controversial people groups and "outsiders". There is no evidence that tongues-speech is necessary evidence of conversion or Spirit-baptism more widely.

To consider tongues-speech more widely would require an in-depth analysis of 1 Cor 12–14, which, neither time nor space allow for in this work. Following the majority of commentators, I can see the possibility that tongues-speech *may* be a private prayer language directing unintelligible utterances toward God.[17] Such a gift, Paul seems to suggest, is better used in private due to its apparently disruptive influence on the assembly.[18] Adding to this the polemical nature of Paul's letter to the Corinthians, and it is difficult to come to certain conclusions regarding the use of such a gift. It appears that the gift Paul is referring to in addressing the Corinthians is possibly analogical, rather than identical, to the intelligible languages understood on the day of Pentecost. Complexities considered, it is probably best, with Paul, not to prohibit tongues-speech, but to restrict it to private devotional use, for the sake of the edification of believers when they gather, and for the sake of visitors who may conclude that "you [believers] are out of your mind" (1 Cor 14:23).[19]

---

17. Ciampa and Rosner, *The First Letter to the Corinthians*, 670–71; Collins, *First Corinthians*, 492; Fee, *The First Epistle to the Corinthians*, 656–57; Thiselton, *The First Epistle to the Corinthians*, 1085–86. Ancient writers who considered tongues-speech still to be in use include Tertullian, *Against Marcion*, 5.8; Novation, *Treatise*; Clement, *Stromata* 4.21.

18. Garland, *1 Corinthians*, 629–30.

19. Further complexities exist in affirming that tongues may be a non-human language. At this point the debate reaches an un-testable impasse and tongues-speech can become a kind of "resistance discourse." (See Smith, "Tongues as 'Resistance Discourse,'" 81–110). For social and psychological issues, as well as tongues-speech in other religions, see *Speaking in Tongues*, ed. Mills; *Speaking in Tongues*, ed. Cartledge.

Acts 2:17–21 in Contemporary Debate

Dreams and Visions

In chapter 1 we observed the close connection between dreams, visions and prophecy, with dreams and visions being the medium through which God often revealed himself to OT prophets. In chapter 3 we noticed that the narrative presentation of dreams and visions serves to direct and vindicate mission (primarily, but not exclusively, Gentile mission), particularly as it pertains to important figures such as Peter and Paul. The repetition of key visions, and the narrative space given to them (e.g. 9:1–18; 10:1–22; 11:4–10; 22:6–18; 26:12–17), testifies to heavenly control over unfolding events. Chronologically, dreams and visions are relatively rare, given the book covers a period of almost thirty years, but in terms of the narrative presentation, the divine authentication of Gentile mission is a clear and regular peal.

Since every believer has the "Spirit of prophecy" and part of the promise for such believers living in the last days includes dreams and visions, we cannot automatically discount a report of a dream or vision thought to be from the Lord. Indeed, there are credible accounts of just such phenomena in the history of the church, ancient and modern. Some of the church fathers considered such things to be operative.[20] John Flavel received a dream prior to embarking on a voyage to London of a storm which accordingly occurred.[21] It might be argued that such instances are better explained in psychological terms, and in some cases this may be true. However, this would not disprove that God might work through such means, on occasion, for his own ends and purposes. Of course, as with the other phenomena under consideration, such a position could lead to unhealthy excess or over-analysis, but given the evidence of Acts, we cannot exclude the possibility that individuals may experience God's providential presence with

---

20. Irenaeus, *Against Heresies*, 2.32.4; Tertullian, *Against Marcion*, 5.8.

21. Flavel, *Works* 1:viii. Similarly, John Newton felt he had been forewarned in a dream regarding a false accusation which was subsequently made against him. Aitken, *John Newton*, 75.

them, on occasion, through dreams or visions. Such occurrences, based on the evidence of Acts and history, are apparently rare, but, from that same evidence, it seems God could still bring comfort or direction by means of dreams and visions—Acts gives us a pattern of sorts, but not a norm.

We will return to consider whether such things constitute a threat to the sufficiency of Scripture. Suffice to say at this juncture, many of these happenings are not in competition to Scripture, but rather apply circumstantially the principles of Scripture.

Signs and Wonders

Third, as argued previously, "signs and wonders" occupy a special place in redemption history and geography. Throughout OT history we observe signs and wonders at significant epochal moments—for example the exodus or the ministry of Elijah and Elisha. It is also worth noting that signs and wonders are often tied to certain key figures in those periods (i.e. Moses in the exodus, Elijah and Elisha, Jesus and the apostles).[22] In Acts, signs and wonders are particularly tied to Jerusalem with all the redemptive history they evoke. To that end they are signs for Israel to recognise the day of the Lord's salvation. They testify to his Messiah and his plan of salvation. There is, therefore, a unique intensity of such phenomena clustered around Jesus and his apostles in the infancy of the church.[23] Hacking is correct to observe that miracles in Acts are not widespread but limited to certain figures and occurring infrequently and sporadically.[24]

22. Warfield, *Counterfeit Miracles,* 22–23.

23. Signs and wonders, as attesting the messengers and the message, is further evidenced in 2 Cor 12:12 and Heb 2:4.

24. Hacking, *Signs and Wonders,* 236. Some Third Wave writers present their narrative of the "third wave" as containing more signs and wonders than any other point in history, including that of Jesus and the apostles. For example see Wagner, *The Third Wave,* 88–100. This may be as much to do with eschatology as pneumatology. Many of these accounts are second-hand or vague, but we must remember that spurious examples do not disprove the

It is also noteworthy that, in Luke's narrative presentation of the miraculous, the occurrences are more frequent in the early stages of the community's formation, and less common as the narrative advances. In narrative terms, the highest proportion of the miraculous occurs in Jerusalem (Acts 1–7); miracles are still present, but proportionately less common as mission expands geographically (Acts 8–15); and are relatively scarce (but not altogether absent) beyond Acts 15. It may be legitimate to conclude that there is a redemptive historical development even within Acts itself.

That said, we see in Acts that signs, wonders, and the miraculous are not confined solely to the twelve, nor Jerusalem, but are also performed by those who are not "apostles" in the narrow sense of the word (e.g. Stephen in Acts 6:8, and Philip in Acts 8:6), and on the frontiers of Gentile mission. Further, it does not necessarily follow logically that the increased intensity of signs and wonders around Jesus and his apostles equals exclusivity. It simply demonstrates the special place they inhabit as authoritative eyewitnesses and messengers, and achieves Luke's narrative aim of reliability.

Therefore, the qualified possibility of ongoing experience of the miraculous is open to us. Some qualifications are as follows.

There does appear to be a redemptive historical development within Acts, and the NT more widely. As Paul entrusts pastoral care to the Ephesian elders (Acts 20:17–38) the emphasis is on shepherding and guarding the flock, and being built up by the "word of his grace" (20:32). Further, as Paul passes on the baton in his letters to Timothy and Titus, there is no mention of signs and wonders—rather they are encouraged to proclaim the apostolic message. As Cole notes the "absence of evidence is not necessarily the evidence of absence," but it does tell us something about the relative emphases of the post-apostolic church.[25] A further deduction, based on the fact that signs and wonders authenticate messengers as well as message, is that where miracles are not required to authenticate

---

existence of the genuine article.

25. Cole, *Engaging with the Holy Spirit*, 82.

messengers, they may still occur in connection with the message. In that case miracles are not so much tied to particular people, but may be performed according to God's sovereign will. This explains why James exhorts the sick to call the elders to pray rather than a particular individual with a gift of healing (Jam 5:14). Gaffin is correct in saying that "the sovereign will and power of God today to heal the sick ... ought to be acknowledged and insisted on."[26]

Pulling these threads together I think the evidence for a *gift* of healing or miraculous powers today is not conclusive. The only reference to such a gift is 1 Cor 12:9–10. Paul simply affirms that some in the apostolic era have such a gift. He does not clearly state such a gift is widespread. All things considered, I would argue that God can heal and perform miracles, but the gift of healing or miraculous powers is not tied permanently to individuals.[27]

Applying some of these thoughts to the contemporary scene I would propose the following: It is unhelpful and probably inappropriate to use the term "signs and wonders" to refer to contemporary miracles due to the particular redemptive-historical use of the phrase. If, as has been argued, the church in its infancy and in its twenty-first century inhabit the same last days, we should expect to see some family resemblances of the church inhabited by the same Spirit. As with dreams and visions, there are excesses and abuses to be avoided, but there are a considerable number of credible accounts of the miraculous throughout the history of the church.[28] Irenaeus and Novation affirm reports of the miraculous as does Augustine who claims to be an eye-witness to one particular healing.[29] Clement acknowledges both the uniqueness

---

26. Gaffin, *Perspectives,* 114.

27. I think it fair to ask, if such a gift were in the church today, should we not expect hospitals to be cleared in a matter of days.

28. Warfield in *Counterfeit Miracles* points out many instances of excess and abuse throughout the history of the church. However, the presence of the imitation necessitates the presence of the genuine.

29. Irenaeus, *Against Heresies* 2.32.4; Novation, *Treatise*; Augustine, *City of God* 22.8. Recounting Augustine's testimony is where Warfield is sadly at his

of the apostles and the continuation of miracles.[30] Bridge in his book, *Signs and Wonders*, claims to have witnessed first-hand a few remarkable healings.[31] Therefore, whilst not encouraging the mindless pursuit of the sensational, or seeking miracles for their own sake, the church corporate should seek and pray expectantly for the Lord's dramatic intervention where appropriate (perhaps for example, in areas such as political or social injustice; persecution of Christians; provision for missionaries and others in need; and for healing) and should expect the Lord to do marvellous things in our day. Of course, God may not answer such prayers in the way we had hoped for, and that is not related to a lack of faith—I wholeheartedly oppose the so called "prosperity gospel". But, suppose a missionary known to us is released unexpectedly from prison after we have prayed, or a friend remarkably recovers from serious illness—is that not God's miraculous intervention? To use a cliché, if it walks like a duck and quacks like a duck, why not call it a duck? To shy away from using "miracle" terminology is a failure to name things rightly, reinforces functional fatalism, discourages a dependent expectancy on the Spirit, and opens up conservatives to the charge of not believing in the miraculous.

---

worst. I hugely appreciate much of Warfield's work, but in *Counterfeit Miracles* his citation of patristic material is selective, conclusions are drawn based on logical fallacies, and his presuppositions dictate his conclusions.

30. Clement, *Stromata* 4.21. Chrysostom argues that the kinds of miracles that were done by the apostles were no longer present (*Homilies on John* 24). The reader must decide upon the reliability of the accounts, but from what I have argued from Acts, I have no strong reason to suppose that *every* account is fictive. To hold to Warfield's position we must conclude that each and every report of the miraculous in the post-apostolic era, without exception, must be of "heathen origin" (*Counterfeit Miracles*, 61). Whereas, to follow the position I am advocating, we only require one example of the genuine article.

31. Bridge, *Signs and Wonders*, 190.

Prophecy

Fourth, and finally, the use of "prophecy" terminology requires reconsideration. As argued in chapter 3, prophecy covers a wide range of phenomena in Acts including preaching, teaching, praise, encouragement, guidance, and even rebuke. Given that all believers possess the "Spirit of prophecy", all believers could, potentially, contribute to the prophetic. That is not the same as saying all have the gift of prophecy. While all possess the Spirit of prophecy and the potential for the prophetic, some may have a particular gifting of prophecy. Part of the problem here is that some charismatics and Pentecostals have hijacked the language of prophecy, and over-emphasized and sensationalized it, such that those of a Reformed or conservative persuasion are reticent to use it. But if what is argued here is correct, then we are engaged in the prophetic already, and much more than we think. We need to recapture the proper use of "prophecy" language, and encourage its use in our various gatherings. In public meetings there could be the space after a sermon for evaluation, question, sharing, and encouragement—some of this may come under the rubric of the "prophetic."[32] Individuals could pass on "impressions" (as the puritans termed them) to elders in the week before a meeting to be discerned and weighed. In homegroups or smaller gatherings, words of encouragement, wisdom, prayer, and teaching may be considered prophetic if they have special insight or are particularly pertinent. This may all sound slightly un-dramatic; that is exactly the point. Reading 1 Cor 14, one of the striking things is just how *un*-sensational it all is.

Some may question here whether the sufficiency of Scripture is undermined. That is a significant and important question. I do not want to be heard as saying that Scripture is not sufficient or

---

32. In conversation with one minister, he recounted how, at a former church, they would have space, after the sermon, if anyone had something they wanted to share. I do not think they would have termed it "prophetic", but I would consider that practice to be what I am advocating here as exercising prophetic ministry.

that we need some extra new revelation to make it complete for our own day. I do believe that Scripture is entirely sufficient addressing all areas of our life directly or by good and necessary implication. Perhaps though, we need to engage, in Frame's terms, in a "higher level of reflection" regarding sufficiency and revelation.[33] The blanket rejection of further revelation falls foul of defining terms too narrowly—i.e. revelation comes to equal special revelation found in the canon of Scripture only. Yet, those of a Reformed persuasion know that God reveals himself every day the sun rises, the rain falls, and crops grow (see for example Acts 14:17; 17:24–31). All of this comes under the title of natural or general revelation.[34] Are there other senses in which God continues to reveal himself? With some careful nuance I believe the answer is both yes and no.[35] God's revelation of his redemptive work in Christ is complete because Christ's work is complete. There will be no new revelation of new stages of redemption (apart from the final *apokalupsis* of Christ). In that sense the objective revelation in Christ and the inspired completed Scripture is final and sufficient. Yet the subjective and existential application of that revelation to individuals in specific contexts, by the Holy Spirit, is happening continuously.[36] In that sense God's revelation is new every day as the Spirit applies redemption to us, changing and transforming us. This is what Paul speaks of in Ephesians 1:17—"I keep asking that the God of our Lord Jesus Christ, the glorious Father, may give you the Spirit of wisdom and revelation, so that you may know him better." If that is not ongoing revelation it is difficult to say what would be.

---

33. Frame's work on this is carefully nuanced and immensely helpful. Much of what follows comes from his work and I am very grateful for it. See Frame, *The Doctrine of the Word of God*, 220–38.

34. Ibid., 234–5.

35. Frame here cites things like dreams, visions, hunches as part of general revelation, with Scripture taking precedence. Ibid., 234.

36. Frame calls this "divine assistance in the application of Scripture." Ibid., 235, n.18.

If Scripture teaches the continuity of such subjective revelation it cannot, by definition, threaten the sufficiency of Scripture.

Further, what do we suppose is happening when we ask God to grant us wisdom to know whether to move buildings, or plant a new church? How does that information come to us? When we pray for the preacher on a Sunday morning that he would speak God's words, how does that happen? When a preacher proclaims a powerful message, is that somehow led and orchestrated by the Spirit?[37] What about the spontaneous and circumstantial application of Scripture in a counselling session? Is it in some sense prophetic? If the semantic range of "prophecy" here advocated is upheld then we must answer in the affirmative.

Poythress introduces further distinctions which are helpful.[38] He argues that Christ is *the* prophet, priest and king, and analogically believers too fulfil those roles (Col 3:16; Eph 2:6; 1 John 3:16).[39] He goes on to argue that the basis for believer's actions may be discursive, non-discursive, or partly discursive.[40] Discursive process would be an explicit awareness of a text of Scripture and exposition of its truth (such as happens in preaching, pastoring, counselling).[41] Non-discursive processes are those which act more on intuition or sense with no awareness of an explicit Scriptural basis for action.[42] Partly discursive is action based partly on intuition, and partly on some parallel situation in Scripture.[43] The

---

37. I remember asking a prominent preacher how he felt his sermon had gone. He responded, "I think we had a little wind in the sails." He would probably not want to term that a prophetic message, but if his self-analysis was correct I think I probably would.

38. Poythress, "Modern Spiritual Gifts," 71–101.

39. Ibid., 71–72.

40. Ibid., 75–76.

41. This is what Peter is doing on the day of Pentecost in Acts 2, and what constitutes much of OT prophetic preaching as the prophets applied and enforced covenantal revelation. See Fee and Stuart, *How to Read,* 165–86.

42. This is perhaps what is happening to Paul and his companions in Acts 16:7–8.

43. The council of Jerusalem's decision in Acts 15 may relate to this

content of each of those processes may be didactic, circumstantial or applicatory. As we engage in these processes today, in the post-apostolic era, we acknowledge that all are fallible and none is "more directly" from the Lord than any other.[44] Often, with mature, well taught, Spirit-indwelt Christians, these more spontaneous circumstantial or applicatory words are the fruit of the Spirit's illumination of special revelation over years or decades in their lives. I do not think that makes it less "prophetic." In fact, that seems to be exactly the point of the New Covenant. A consequence of the presence of the Spirit, writing law on hearts, and the democratization of access to God, is that all believers have access to, and can communicate God's truth.[45] The authority of such communications is only insofar as they conform to Scripture. Scripture remains the only infallible authoritative word. Our words our mixed, fallible and therefore not authoritative as Scripture is. Grudem helpfully outlines this as follows:

> We must insist that God does not require us to believe anything about himself or his work in the world which is contained in . . . [such] revelations but not in Scripture. And we must insist that God does not require us to obey any moral directives which come to us through such means but are not confirmed by Scripture.[46]

Someone may bring a word of profound insight, understanding or wisdom, which may shape individual or church life, but it must not be seen as being binding or authoritative. The appropriation of such "prophecies" requires wisdom and discernment, bringing all things to the bar of Scripture.

---

category.

44. Ibid., 79–83.

45. This is the view of Calvin and Stott as they interpret Acts 2:17. Where I wish to go beyond their definition is in affirming that some may have particular gifting in discerning and communicating this truth, as do others with regard to priestly or kingly functions.

46. Grudem, *Prophecy,* 306.

THE POWER OF PENTECOST

So far much of what I have argued ties the "prophetic" closely to special revelation, in the sense of being some sort of application of Scripture. What about insight into unknown situations or predictive prophecies like those of Agabus? On the evidence of Acts such words are rare in time and scope, and Luke is not giving us a pattern to follow. Further, 1 Corinthians speaks of "wise" and "knowing" words but we cannot be sure that is the same as the kind of unknowable insight practised by many today.[47] I do not think Scripture prohibits contemporary instances of prediction or special insight, but if they occur they are unusual, need careful weighing (1 Cor 14:29; 1 Thess 5:21; 1 John 4:1), and are not binding.[48]

Perhaps a further distinction may help here. Perhaps it is helpful to distinguish between capital 'P' prophecy and small 'p' prophecy. Admittedly, put this way, it is not a distinction found in Scripture, but the semantic range of *propheteuo* encourages the distinction. Capital 'P' prophecy is the inscripturated words of the prophet, such as is mentioned in Eph 2:20, and 2 Pet 1:19–21. Small 'p' prophecy is the kind of activity seen in Acts including encouragement, powerful preaching, rebuke and prayer. This is where Gaffin's understanding is too narrow. I agree with his inter-

---

47. See for example the kinds of things advocated by Johnson and Clark in *Essential Guide to Healing*. In 1 Cor 12:8, wisdom (σοφίας) and knowledge (γνώσεως) are adjectival modifiers of the noun λόγος (word) and may therefore be translated simply as a "wise word" or a "knowing word."

48. This is perhaps the area where, in practice, I have most difficulty with some charismatic practice. Such words are incredibly frequent, occurring multiple times in a single meeting, treated as binding, and never (in my experience) tested. I recently saw a man invite for prayer someone who had pain in the hip. As it turned out, nobody present acknowledged such a problem. Nobody confessed that such a word was not from the Lord. I read a case recently of a lady bringing a vision to her church leaders of an over-crowded forest. This vision was taken to approve the joining of two fellowships. Was this from the Lord? Possibly, but since the subject is fallible, it cannot be authoritative, and must itself be subject to scriptural teaching and principles. Such a word may be a providential confirmation of a plan, but one would not want to base the direction of a church solely on such visions.

Acts 2:17–21 in Contemporary Debate

pretation of Eph 2:20—that the authoritative foundational prophets are NT prophets. That is, I believe, the correct understanding of that particular instance of the use of the word προφήτης.[49] However, Gaffin goes on to make this particular use of the word the controlling definition such that all other instances in the NT are required to fit into the same narrow definition.[50] This displays a lack of sensitivity to the semantic range and linguistic extension of the word.[51] We could pick other NT words like ἐκκλησία (church), ἁγιάζω/ἁγιασμὸς (sanctify), or δίκαιος/δικαιόω (righteousness) and make the same mistake.[52] Words are used with a breadth of potential meaning. Context determines the intention of a word. As already argued, prophecy covers a range of things within Acts (and within the NT) such that we can, on the one hand, say there are no more Eph 2:20 prophets, yet, on the other, affirm the continuation of the prophetic on all those who possess the Spirit of prophecy (namely, every believer).[53] This may not be as neat and systematized as we might like, but the alternative is to disavow ourselves

---

49. So too Hoehner, *Ephesians*, 400–401; Lincoln, *Ephesians*, 152–53; O'Brien, *Ephesians*, 214–16; Thielman, *Ephesians*, 180–81.

50. Gaffin, *Perspectives*, 96. Gaffin is open to "spontaneous Spirit-worked application of Scripture ... [to] a particular situation or problem" (120), which demonstrates that much of this debate is about appropriate terminology.

51. O'Brien notes the semantic range of the prophet/prophecy word group within the NT allows for different kinds of prophecy. *Ephesians*, 215.

52. Bannerman notes five different senses of the word ἐκκλησία, including universal, local, triumphant and militant (*Church of Christ* 1.5–17). Holiness words (ἁγιάζω/ἁγιασμὸς) can carry a sense of definitive or progressive sanctification (compare Rom 6:19 with 1 Cor 1:2); Procksch, "ἁγιάζω" *TDNT* 1:88–115. Righteousness words (δίκαιος/δικαιόω) also have a semantic range (compare for example Luke 1:6 with Rom 3:10); Schrenk, "δίκαιος" *TDNT* 2.174–225.

53. If this distinction holds, nobody today should preface their speech with "thus says the Lord." That is to claim more authority than the NT would permit. Even the preacher expounding a text cannot utter those words, with regards his own words, since his own words may contain some error. Perhaps better prefacing might include words such as "sense," "feel," or "think." Further, the more public the word, the greater the need for public weighing.

of the language completely and thus, fail to name things rightly, and leave ourselves open to the charge of not believing or practicing some of these things.[54] I recognize there are pastoral concerns and implications. Where might it all end if we start using the "p" word in our meetings? It will require strong leadership and clear thinking and teaching, but this it seems to me is the most biblical ground to proceed on based on what I understand of Acts 2 (and the NT more widely). Somebody may ask how this alters what we already do—what is the practical difference? I would reply that, first we are being more faithful to Christ and the Scriptures to use the terminology and vocabulary he has given us; and second we do recover a greater sense of dependence upon, sensitivity to, and responsiveness of and to the *person* who lives inside and among us—the person we seem practically to forget and exclude in most of our times together (at least those of us from more conservative or Reformed churches).

Hopefully these preliminary musings may begin to address how I might put some of these things into practice.

CONCLUSION

In this chapter I have attempted to provide a third way through the debate over the continuation of the charismata, by considering the narrative *as* narrative. This involves taking into consideration Luke's authorial intent, seen through a number of rhetorical strategies, and considering the Spirit's role in Luke's overall project. This has served to demonstrate that Acts 2:17–21 is part of Luke's strategy authenticating Jesus as the exalted Davidic Messiah, now ruling over "Israel" in her new exodus and restoration.

---

54. I visited a couple recently who asked why we did not, as a church, practice prophecy. In those situations I inevitably feel awkward, either because the questioner may be slightly confrontational, or because I have to make a long winded, almost embarrassed, apology for our position. It would be liberating to answer "yes, we do, and this is what it is really about."

Whilst we may not be permitted to extrapolate norms regarding charismatic practice, we do see consistent patterns in the book of Acts. The Christian community in Acts experiences prophecies, dreams and visions, and signs and wonders. Undoubtedly these play a specific function within Luke's narrative, but the Spirit which characterized the early believers is the same person who dwells among and characterizes the church in subsequent generations. Therefore, whilst there may be an increased intensity, particularly in narrative presentation, of such phenomena in the book of Acts, it would seem unwarranted to argue for the complete cessation of such phenomena. The promise of Acts 2:17–21 crosses social and temporal boundaries—it is a promise for all without distinction, and while recognising the special narrative function of the Holy Spirit in Acts, and Luke's emphasis on the restoration of Israel in her new exodus, I would expect to see some "family-resemblances" in the church throughout varying global and historical positions.[55] As a tentative suggestion, it may be that cultures resembling Ephesus, placing high value on magic (like modern-day Africa or Asia) may see an increased amount of demon-possession or the miraculous.[56] Also, perhaps those on the frontiers of mission may see more dramatic in-breakings of eschatological realities.

When we appreciate Acts for what it is—a *narrative*—we can begin to take a more moderate approach to the contemporary

55. On the issue of expectation, Sinclair Ferguson, a cessationist open to the possibility of providential healings and miracles, says "that healing is much more frequent among continuationists than among cessationists … may not lie in the interpretative grid adopted but in the faith which seeks (and may even anticipate) the intervention of God. Ferguson, *Holy Spirit*, 236.

56. This is not the same as a belief in territorial spirits (but see Deut 32:8–9 LXX). This is rather the suggestion that some cultures are more given over to demon worship, and consequently spiritual warfare is experienced more intensely and more miracles are observed. To some degree it seems the experience of the miraculous may be linked to expectation and fervency of prayer. This is at least the experience of the missionary James Fraser, who worked in the Yunnan province in the early part of the 20th century. For an account of his work and experience see Lowe, *Territorial Spirits and World Evangelisation?* 130–50.

debates. The normative intent of Luke to provide certainty regarding the claims of gospel is non-negotiable—the way of salvation through Christ is a norm. Questions of ecclesiological or missional praxis must appeal to patterns which may or may not be repeatable. Simply put, we must do the hard-yards of exegesis in each case, rather than looking for proof-texts or systems that fail to read Acts as a narrative. Perhaps, this conclusion is less than satisfying, but, as I hope has been demonstrated, the extremes within Pentecostalism and cessationism fail to engage Luke's work as a narrative with the result that their conclusions are too problematic to be accepted uncritically.

Conclusion

IN THE introduction we noted that the contemporary debate over charismatic practice was as important as it is sometimes heated. We also noted the role Acts plays in that debate with Acts 2:17-21 being a *crux interpretum*. What this book has attempted, is a careful analysis of the text in its immediate and wider context, as a means of bringing more light and less heat to the discussion. The text of Acts 2:17-21 has been analysed as follows:

In chapter 1 we undertook an exegesis of Acts 2:17-21, examining the grammar, syntax and meaning of the verses, paying particular attention to changes made to the LXX of Joel 3:1-5. Preliminary thoughts on the phenomena mentioned were offered and three pertinent observations on the text emerged. First, the insertion of the redemptively significant ἐν ταῖς ἐσχάταις ἡμέραις (in the last days) to the LXX has the effect of uniting first-generation Christians with subsequent generations of believers. Contemporary Christians still inhabit the last days; therefore the promise (however we understand it) still stands. Second, we observed the addition of προφητεύσουσιν in v. 18. This double occurrence of προφητεύσουσιν (vv. 17-18) demonstrates the importance of prophecy for Luke as all believers now possess the "Spirit of prophecy." Third, we observed the socio-economic and gender democratization of the Spirit as young and old, male and female, slave and free are included as recipients of the promised blessing.

In chapter 2 we examined Acts 2:17-21 in the context of Acts 1-2. We noted a number of significant OT allusions and motifs, and argued that Luke is presenting, in the early chapters of his narrative, the restoration of Israel in her new exodus. The reconstitution of the twelve, the reversal of Babel at the new Sinai, and the restoration of the Davidic throne and King fulfil OT prophetic hope as the climax of Israel's story. Thus there is something uniquely constitutive and unrepeatable about the events of Acts 2.

In chapter 3 we saw the ways in which Acts 2:17–21 is programmatic for, and fulfilled in, the subsequent narrative. The presence of prophecy, dreams and visions, and signs and wonders in the subsequent narrative all serve to demonstrate that the "restoration of Israel" is underway on a significant scale. The various phenomena are not just evidential however—they are also the means by which "Israel" is restored and fulfils her commission to be a light to the nations (1:8). While the *events* of Acts 2 are unique, the *promise* is still being worked out. The rest of Acts is the overflow of that which was poured out at Pentecost.

In chapter 4 we moved to consider Acts 2:17–21 within Luke's wider project. We began by noting that any discussion of "normativity" must consider authorial intent, and defended authorial intent as a legitimate and worthy aim. We examined Luke's intent—to provide ἀσφάλεια (certainty) for his reader, his literary strategies toward that rhetorical end, and we observed the Spirit's role in that endeavour. In exploring Luke's aim we noted the dangers of reading paradigms for practice from the narrative where such things were not the *primary* intent of the author.

In chapter 5 we moved to consider Acts 2:17–21 in the contemporary charismatic debate. Being aware of the dangers associated with looking for norms, we took note of Fee's helpful distinction between norms and patterns, and concluded that while we may not be permitted to draw norms regarding the phenomena described in Acts 2:17–21, we do see patterns, which may be repeatable in subsequent generations characterised by the Spirit. I offered some thoughts on what these Spirit-characterised family resemblances may look like.

Examining the text in these ever widening concentric circles has served to demonstrate the twofold thesis proposed. First, Acts 2:17–21 exists in a literary context which seeks to show how

Conclusion

Israel's story has reached its climax. Luke's narrative portrays these historic events (that is the events of Luke-Acts) as the restoration of Israel in her new exodus. Thus, Pentecost is a climactic constitutive salvation-historical event and is therefore unique and unrepeatable, *as a historical event*. Second, whilst the Pentecost event is uniquely constitutive, this does not mean that the *phenomena* described in Acts 2 are unrepeatable. The promise still stands and is being worked out. The church inhabits the same "last days", and is characterized by the same Spirit,[1] and the various work of the Spirit is clearly seen throughout Acts. The contemporary church ought to expect to see some family similarities of all those led by the Spirit—this includes, I suggest, some evidence of these charismatic phenomena. Prophecy, in its variegated forms, is characteristic of the new community indwelt and empowered by the Spirit. Dreams and visions serve to direct and assure missionary endeavour. Signs and wonders are particularly linked to Jerusalem with all the OT history they evoke, but the miraculous may be a repeatable aspect of the early church's experience. As Turner notes, the intensity today may be less than that of the first generation of the church, due in part to the legitimizing function of signs and wonders for the apostles, and the as yet unclosed canon.[2] Still, the promise of Acts 2:17–21 remains a promise for the last days—a promise which transcends temporal, social and geographical boundaries.[3]

The foregoing argument serves to challenge contemporary churches in a variety of ways. First, I am not persuaded that some of those presenting the cessationist case have sufficiently wrestled with the exegesis of Acts 2:17–21. In particular they have failed to grapple with what it means for the promise to be for *all* in the "last days."

Second, conservative churches need to put theology into practice. Many conservatives would support the exegesis pro-

---

1. Carson, *Showing the Spirit*, 151.
2. Turner, *Holy Spirit and Spiritual Gifts*, 301.
3. Ruthven, *On Cessation*, 125.

posed here but would remain *in practice* cessationist. The fact that some of the terminology (of Acts 2:17–21) has been hijacked, and some of the claims appear to have been bogus, does not require conservatives (and I here include myself) to over-react in the other direction. The Reformation restored the threefold office of prophet, priest, and king to every believer. Those of us that follow in their footsteps have embraced the priesthood of every believer, and to some degree the kingly leader functions entrusted to every believer. We need to work towards recovering the prophethood of every believer.

Third, charismatic and Pentecostal churches are in need of a more robust biblical theology and hermeneutic. To simply appropriate the promise of Acts 2:17–21 as paradigmatic is to miss the climactic redemptive-historical moment and misunderstand its purpose in Luke's literary endeavour. Further, some practices are not in line with careful exegesis of Scripture, and in some cases have no biblical warrant whatsoever.[4]

While this work proposes a middle way through the debate, what is clearly needed is further work in the area of applied hermeneutics. Further research into how to determine norms or paradigms in narrative would help to make some significant progress in this debate. In addition, some careful and applied thinking about how the conclusions of this book may be put into practice in a local church is required—particularly given the British ecclesiastical scene sadly has more bad examples than good. What is clear is that much more work needs to be done. Hopefully this short study can make some small contribution to the ongoing discussion.

---

4. For example much of the phenomena associated with the so called "Toronto Blessing" is lacking in any biblical warrant. Such activity included uncontrollable laughter, shaking, roaring, and being "slain in the Spirit". While somewhat *passé* these practices can still be observed in contemporary churches.

Bibliography

Aitken, Jonathan. *John Newton: From Disgrace to Amazing Grace.* London: Continuum, 2007.

Alexander, Loveday. ""Septuaginta, Fachprosa, Imitatio: Albert Wifstrand and the Language of Luke-Acts"." Pages 231–52 in *Acts In Its Ancient Literary Context.* Edited by Loveday Alexander. Edited by Loveday Alexander. LNTS 298. London: T. & T. Clark, 2005.

———. ""This is That": The Authority of Scripture in the Acts of the Apostles." Pages 55–72 in *History and Exegesis.* Edited by Sang-Won Son. London: T. & T. Clark, 2006.

———. *Acts In Its Ancient Literary Context.* Edited by Loveday Alexander. LNTS 298. London: T. & T. Clark, 2005.

Aristotle. *On Rhetoric.* Translated by George A. Kennedy. Oxford: Oxford University Press, 2007.

Aune, David E. *Prophecy in Early Christianity and the Ancient Mediterranean World.* Eerdmans: Grand Rapids, 1983.

Austin, J.L. *How To Do Things With Words.* Oxford: Oxford University Press, 1962.

Balz, H. "τεσσεράκοντα," In *TDNT* 8:136.

Barrett, C.K. *A Critical and Exegetical Commentary on the Acts of the Apostles.* ICC. Volume 1. London: T. & T. Clark International, 1994.

Barrett, C.K. *A Critical and Exegetical Commentary on the Acts of the Apostles.* ICC. Volume 2. London: T. & T. Clark International, 1998.

Bauckham, Richard. *Jesus and The Eyewitnesses: The Gospels as Eyewitness Testimony.* Grand Rapids: Eerdmans, 2006.

Beale, G.K. "The Descent of the Eschatological Temple in the Form of the Spirit at Pentecost: Part 1: The Clearest Evidence." *TynB* 56(1): 73–102.

Behm, J. "γλῶσσα," In *TDNT* 1:724.

Betz, O. "φωνῇ" In *TDNT* 9:296.

Billington, Anthony, Tony Lane, and Max Turner, eds. *Mission and Meaning.* Carlisle: Paternoster, 1995.

Blass, F. and A. Debrunner. *A Greek Grammar of the New Testament and Other Early Christian Literature.* Translated and revised by Robert W. Funk. Cambridge: Cambridge University Press, 1961.

Bock, Darrell L. *Acts.* BECNT. Grand Rapids: Baker, 2007.

———. *Luke 1:1–9:50.* BECNT. Grand Rapids: Baker, 1994.

———. *Proclamation From Prophecy and Pattern: Lucan Old Testament Christology.* JSNTSup 12. Sheffield: Sheffield Academic Press, 1987.

Bonnah, George K. A. *The Holy Spirit: A Narrative Factor in the Acts of the Apostles.* SBB 58. Stuttgart: Verlag Katholisches Bibelwerk GmbH, 2007.

Bridge, Donald. *Signs and Wonders.* Leicester: Inter-Varsity Press, 1985.

Brodie, Thomas L. "Luke-Acts as an Imitation and Emulation of the Elijah-Elisha Narrative." Pages 78–85 in *New Views on Luke and Acts.* Edited by Earl Richard. Collegeville, Minn.: Liturgical Press, 1990.

Bromiley, Geoffrey W., ed. *Theological Dictionary of the New Testament.* 10 vols. Grand Rapids: Eerdmans, 1964.

Brown, Colin, ed. *New International Dictionary of New Testament Theology.* 4 vols. Grand Rapids: Zondervan, 1975–1985.

Brown, C. and C.H. Peisker, "Prophet" In *NIDNTT* 3:87

Bruce, F.F. *The Acts of the Apostles: Greek Text with Introduction and Commentary.* 3rd revised and enlarged ed. Leicester: Apollos, 1990.

Bruner, Frederick Dale. *A Theology of the Holy Spirit: The Pentecostal Experience and the New Testament Witness.* London: Hodder & Stoughton, 1970.

Bultmann, R. "ἐπιγινώσκω" in *TDNT* 1:689–719.

Cadbury, H.J. "Commentary on the Preface of Luke." Pages 489–510 in *The Acts of the Apostles.* Edited by F.J. Foakes-Jackson and K. Lake. Vol. 2 of *The Beginnings of Christianity.* London: Macmillan and Co., 1922.

Calvin, John. *Commentary upon the Acts of the Apostles.* Translated by Christopher Fetherstone. 1585. Repr., Grand Rapids: Baker Book House, 1998.

———. *Institutes of the Christian Religion.* Edited by John T. McNeill. Translated by Ford Lewis Battles. 2 Vols. Library of Christian Classics XX-XXI. Philadelphia: Westminster Press, 1960.

Carson, D.A. *Showing the Spirit: A Theological Exposition of 1 Corinthians 12–14.* Grand Rapids: Baker, 1987.

———. *The Gagging of God: Christianity Confronts Pluralism.* Leicester: Apollos, 1996.

Carson, D.A. and G.K. Beale, eds. *Commentary on the New Testament Use of the Old Testament.* Grand Rapids: Baker Academic, 2007.

Cartledge, Mark J. ed. *Speaking in Tongues: Multi-Disciplinary Perspectives.* Milton Keynes: Paternoster, 2006.

Charlesworth, James H., ed. *Apocalyptic Literature and Testaments*. Vol. 1 of *The Old Testament Pseudepigrapha*. NY.: Doubleday, 1982.

———. *Expansions of the Old Testament and Legends, Wisdom and Philosophical Literature, Prayers, Psalms, and Odes, Fragments of Lost Judeo-Hellenistic Works*. Vol. 2 of *The Old Testament Pseudepigrapha*. NY.: Doubleday, 1982.

Ciampa, Roy E., and Brian S. Rosner, *The First Letter to the Corinthians*. PNTC. Grand Rapids: Eerdmans, 2010.

Cole, Graham A. *Engaging with the Holy Spirit*. Nottingham: Apollos, 2007.

Collins, Raymond F. *First Corinthians*. SP 7. Collegeville, Minn.: Liturgical, 1999.

Conzelmann, Hans. *Acts of the Apostles*. Hermeneia. Philadelphia: Fortress, 1987.

Cosgrove, Charles H. "The Divine DEI in Luke-Acts." *NovT* 26 (1984) 168–90.

Danker, Frederick William, ed. *A Greek-English Lexicon of the New Testament and other Early Christian Literature*. 3rd ed. 1957. Repr., Chicago: Chicago University Press, 2000.

Darr, John A. *Herod the Fox: Audience Criticism and Lukan Characterisation*. JSNTSup 163. Sheffield: Sheffield Academic Press, 1998.

———. *On Character Building: The Reader and the Rhetoric of Characterization in Luke-Acts*. Louisville, Ky.: Westminster John Knox, 1992.

Deere, J. *Surprised by the Voice of God*. Eastbourne: Kingsway, 1996.

———. *Surprised by the Power of the Spirit*. Eastbourne: Kingsway, repr. 2000.

Denaux, A. & R. Corstjens. *The Vocabulary of Luke*. Biblical Tools and Studies 10. Leuven: Peeters, 2009.

Dillon, R.J. "Previewing Luke's Project from his Prologue." *CBQ* 43 (1981): 205–27.

Doyle, R., ed. *Signs and Wonders and Evangelicals*. Randburg: Fabel, 1987.

Dunn, James D. G. "Baptism in the Spirit: A Response to Pentecostal Scholarship on Luke-Acts." *JPT* 3 (1993): 3–27.

———. *Baptism in the Holy Spirit*. Studies in Biblical Theology 15. London: SCM, 1970.

———. *Beginning From Jerusalem*. Christianity in the Making. Vol 2. Eerdmans: Grand Rapids, 2009.

———. *The Acts of the Apostles*. Epworth Commentaries. Peterborough: Epworth Press, 1996.

Dupont, J. "Ascension du Christ et don de l'Esprit d'apres Actes 2:33." Pages 219–28 in *Christ and Spirit in the New Testament. Studies in honour of Charles Francis Digby Moule*. Edited by B Lindars and S. S. Smalley. Cambridge: Cambridge University Press, 1973.

Elbert, Paul, ed. *Essays on Apostolic Themes.* Peabody, Mass.: Hendrickson, 1985.
Ellis, E. Earle. "The Role of the Christian Prophet in Acts." Pages 55–67 in *Apostolic History and the Gospel: Biblical and Historical Essays Presented to F.F.Bruce.* Edited by W. Ward Gasque and Ralph P. Martin. Exeter: Paternoster, 1970.
———. "Quotations (in the New Testament)." In *NBD,* 995.
Evans, Craig A. "The Prophetic Setting of the Pentecost Sermon." *ZNW* 74 (1983): 148–50.
Evans, C.F. *Saint Luke.* NTC. London: SCM, 1990.
Evans, Mary J. "The Prophethood of all Believers." Pages 31–40 in *Mission and Meaning.* Edited by Anthony Billington, Tony Lane, and Max Turner. Carlisle: Paternoster, 1995.
Fee, Gordon D. *Gospel and Spirit: Issues in New Testament Hermeneutics.* Peabody, Mass.: Hendrickson, 1991.
———. *The First Epistle to the Corinthians.* NICNT. Grand Rapids: Eerdmans, 1987.
Ferguson, Sinclair B. *The Holy Spirit.* Contours of Christian Theology. Leicester: Inter-Varsity Press, 1996.
Fernando, Ajith. *Acts.* NIVAC. Grand Rapids: Zondervan, 1998.
Fitzmyer, J. A. "The Role of the Spirit in Luke-Acts." Pages 165–84 in *The Unity of Luke-Acts.* Edited by J. Verheyden. Leuven: Leuven University Press, 1999.
———. *The Acts of the Apostles.* AB 31. NY.: Doubleday, 1998.
———. *The Gospel According to Luke I-IX.* AB 28. NY.: Doubleday, 1979.
Flavel, John. *The Works of John Flavel.* 6 vols. London: Banner of Truth, repr. 1968.
Foakes-Jackson, F.J. and K. Lake, eds. *The Acts of the Apostles.* Vol. 2 of *The Beginnings of Christianity.* London: Macmillan and Co., 1922.
Frame, John M. *The Doctrine of the Word of God.* Philipsburg, NJ.: P&R, 2010.
Freedman, David Noel, ed. *The Anchor Bible Dictionary.* 6 vols. NY.: Doubleday, 1992.
Frein, Brigid Curtin. "Narrative Predictions, Old Testament Prophecies and Luke's Sense of Fulfilment." *NTS* 40 (1994): 23–37.
Friedrich, G. and R. Meyer, "προφήτης" In *TDNT* 6:797–852.
Gadamer, Hans-Georg. *Truth and Method.* Translation edited by Garrett Barden and John Cumming. London: Sheed & Ward, 1975.
Gaffin, Richard B. "A Cessationist View." Pages 23–64 in *Are Miraculous Gifts for Today.* Edited by Wayne Grudem. Leicester: Inter-Varsity Press, 1996.
———. *Perspectives on Pentecost.* Phillipsburg, NJ.: P&R, 1979.

Gallagher, Robert L. and Paul Hertig, eds. *Mission in Acts.* NY.: Orbis Books, 2004.

Garland, David E. *1 Corinthians.* BECNT. Grand Rapids: Baker, 2003.

Gasque, W. Ward and Ralph P. Martin, eds. *Apostolic History and the Gospel: Biblical and Historical Essays Presented to F.F.Bruce.* Exeter: Paternoster, 1970.

Gaventa, Beverly Roberts. *Acts.* ANTC. Nashville, Tenn.: Abingdon, 2003.

———. "Toward a Theology of Acts." *Interpretation* 42 (1988): 146–57.

Gilbert, Gary. "From Eschatology to Imperialism: Mapping the Territory of Acts 2." Pages 84–110 in *The Gospels According to Michael Goulder.* Edited by Christopher A. Rollston. Harrisburg, Penn.: Trinity, 2002.

Gill, David W.J. and Conrad Gempf, eds. *Graeco-Roman Setting.* BAIIFCS. Vol 2. Grand Rapids: Eerdmans, 1994.

Gooding, David. *True to the Faith: A Fresh Approach to the Acts of the Apostles.* London: Hodder & Stoughton, 1990.

Goodman, Martin. *Rome and Jerusalem: The Clash of Ancient Civilizations.* London: Penguin, 2007.

Green, Chris. *The Word of His Grace: A guide to teaching and preaching from Acts.* Leicester: Inter-Varsity Press, 2005.

Green, Joel B. ""In Our Own Languages": Pentecost, Babel, and the Shaping of Christian Community in Acts 2:1–13." Pages 198–213 in *The Word Leaps the Gap: Essays on Scripture and Theology in honor of Richard B. Hays.* Edited by J. Ross Wagner, C. Kavin Rowe, and Katherine Grieb. Grand Rapids: Eerdmans, 2008.

———. "Salvation to the End of the Earth: God as the Saviour in the Acts of the Apostles." Pages 83–106 in *Witness to the Gospel.* Edited by I. Howard Marshall and David Peterson. Grand Rapids: Eerdmans, 1998.

Green, Michael. *I Believe in the Holy Spirit.* London: Hodder and Stoughton, 1975.

Grudem, Wayne. *The Gift of Prophecy in the New Testament and Today.* revised ed. Wheaton, IL.: Crossway, 2000.

———, ed. *Are Miraculous Gifts for Today.* Leicester: Inter-Varsity Press, 1996.

Hackenberg, "ἐπιγινώσκω" *EDNT* 2:24–25.

Hacking, Keith J. *Signs and Wonders Then and Now.* Nottingham: Apollos, 2006.

Haenchen, Ernst. *The Acts of the Apostles.* Translated by R. McL. Wilson. Oxford: Blackwell, 1971.

Hamilton, James M. Jr. *God's Indwelling Presence: The Holy Spirit in the Old & New Testaments.* NAC Studies in Bible & Theology. Nashville, Tenn.: B&H Academic, 2006.

Hardon, John A. "The Miracle Narratives in the Acts of the Apostles." *CBQ* 16 (1954): 303–18.

Hays, Richard B. "The Liberation of Israel in Luke-Acts: Intertextual Narration as Countercultural Practice." Pages 101–117 in *Reading the Bible Intertextually*. Edited by Richard B. Hays, Stefan Alkier, and Leroy A. Huizenga. Waco, Tex.: Baylor Univ. Press, 2009.

Hays, Richard B., Stefan Alkier, and Leroy A. Huizenga, eds. *Reading the Bible Intertextually*. Waco, Tex.: Baylor Univ. Press, 2009.

Helyer, Larry R. "Luke and the Restoration of Israel." *JETS* 36.3 (1993): 317–29.

Hengel, Martin. *Acts and the History of Earliest Christianity*. Translated by John Bowden. London: SCM Press, 1979.

Hill, David. *New Testament Prophecy*. London: Marshall, Morgan, Scott, 1979.

———. "The Spirit and the Church's Witness: Observations on Acts 1:6–8." *IBS* 6 (1984): 16–26.

Hoehner, Harold H. *Ephesians*. Grand Rapids: Baker, 2002.

Homer. *The Odyssey*. Vol. 454 of *Everyman's Library*. Translated by William Cowper. London: Dent & Sons, 1910.

Hunter, Harold. "Tongues-Speech: A Patristic Analysis." *JETS* 23.2 (1980): 125–37.

Hur, Ju. *A Dynamic Reading of the Holy Spirit in Luke-Acts*. JSNTSup 211. Sheffield: Sheffield Academic Press, 2001.

Jensen, Peter F. "Calvin, Charismatics and Miracles." *EQ* 51 (1979): 131–144.

Jervell, Jacob. *Luke and the People of God*. Minneapolis, Minn.: Augsburg, 1972.

———. *The Theology of the Acts of the Apostles*. Cambridge: CUP, 1996.

Johnson, B., and R. Clark. *Essential Guide to Healing*. Grand Rapids: Chosen, 2011. No Pages. Online: http://books.google.co.uk/books?id=ktageZChnQcC&printsec=frontcover#v=onepage&q&f=false.

Johnson, Luke Timothy. *The Acts of the Apostles*. SP 5. Collegeville, Minn.: The Liturgical Press, 1992.

———. *The Gospel of Luke*. Edited by Daniel J. Harrington. SP 3. Collegeville, Minn.: The Liturgical Press, 1991.

Jordan, James B. *Through New Eyes: Developing a Biblical View of the World*. Eugene, Oregon: Wipf & Stock, 1999.

Josephus. Translated by H. St. J. Thackeray et al. 10 vols. LCL. Cambridge: Harvard University Press, 1926–1965.

Käsemann, Ernst. *Essays on New Testament Themes*. SBT 41. London: SCM, 1964.

Kavin Rowe, C. *World Upside Down: Reading Acts in its Graeco-Roman Context*. Oxford: Oxford University Press, 2009.

Keck, Leander, ed. *Acts, Romans, 1 Corinthians*. Vol. X of *The New Interpreter's Bible*. Edited by Leander Keck. Nashville, Tenn.: Abingdon, 2002.

Keener, Craig S. "Why Does Luke Use Tongues as a Sign of the Spirit's Empowerment." *J* 15.2 (2007): 177–84.

———. *Gift & Giver: The Holy Spirit for Today*. Grand Rapids: Baker, 2001.

Kelsey, Morton T. *Healing and Christianity*. London: SCM, 1973.

Kik, J. Marcellus. *An Eschatology of Victory*. Phillipsburg, NJ.: P&R, 1971.

Koehler, L., Baumgartner, W., and Johann Stamm. *The Hebrew and Aramaic Lexicon of the Old Testament*. Translated and edited under supervision of M.E.J. Richardson. 5 vols. Leiden: Brill, 2001.

Koet, Bart J. "Divine Communication in Luke-Acts." Pages 745–57 in *The Unity of Luke-Acts*. Edited by J. Verheyden. Leuven: Leuven University Press, 1999.

Köstenberger, Andreas. "What does it mean to be filled with the Spirit? A Biblical Investigation." *JETS* 40.2 (1997): 229–40.

Kremer, J., ed. *Les Actes Des Apôtres: Traditions, Rédaction, Théologie*. Leuven: Leuven University Press, 1979.

Lampe, G.W.H. "Miracles in the Acts of the Apostles." Pages 165–78 in *Miracles*. Edited by C.F.D Moule. Cambridge Studies in their Philosophy and History. London: A.R.Mowbray and Co Ltd., 1965.

———. *The Seal of the Spirit*. London: Longmans, Green & Co., 1951.

Larkin Jr., William J. *Acts*. The IVP New Testament Commentary Series. Downers Grove, Ill.: IVP, 1995.

Lee, Mark. "An Evangelical Dialogue on Luke, Salvation and Spirit Baptism." *Pneuma* 26.1 (2004): 81–98.

Liddell, Henry George and Robert Scott, eds. *A Greek-English Lexicon*. Oxford: Clarendon, 1968.

Lincoln, Andrew T. *Ephesians*. WBC 42. Dallas, Tex.: Word, 1990.

Lindars, B and S. S. Smalley, eds. *Christ and Spirit in the New Testament. Studies in honour of Charles Francis Digby Moule*. Cambridge: Cambridge University Press, 1973.

Lindblom, J. *Prophecy in Ancient Israel*. Oxford: Blackwell, 1978.

Litwak, Kenneth Duncan. *Echoes of Scripture in Luke-Acts*. JSNTSup 282. Sheffield: Sheffield Academic Press, 2005.

Longenecker, Richard N. *Acts of the Apostles*. Vol. 9 of *The Expositor's Bible Commentary*. Edited by Frank E. Gaebelein. Grand Rapids: Zondervan, 1981.

———. *Biblical Exegesis in the Apostolic Period*. Grand Rapids: Eerdmans, 1999.

Louw, J.P. and E.A. Nida, eds. *Greek-English Lexicon of the New Testament: Based on Semantic Domains. Edited by J. P. Louw and E. A. Nida*. 2nd ed. 2 vols. NY.: United Bible Societies, 1989.

MacArthur Jr., John F. *Charismatic Chaos*. Grand Rapids: Zondervan, 1992.

Maddox, Robert. *The Purpose of Luke-Acts*. Edinburgh: T. & T. Clark, 1992.

Maile, John F. "The Ascension in Luke-Acts." *TynB* 37 (1986): 29–59.

Marshall, I. Howard. *Luke: Historian and Theologian*. Grand Rapids: Zondervan, 1970.

———. *The Acts of the Apostles: An Introduction and Commentary*. TNTC 5. Leicester: Inter-Varsity Press, 1980.

Marshall, I. Howard and David Peterson, eds. *Witness to the Gospel*. Grand Rapids: Eerdmans, 1998.

Martinson, Paul Varo. "The Ending is Prelude." Pages 313–23 in *Mission in Acts*. Edited by Robert L. Gallagher and Paul Hertig. NY.: Orbis Books, 2004.

Masters, Peter and John C. Whitcomb. *The Charismatic Phenomenon*. 1982. Repr., London: The Wakeman Trust, 1992.

Maxwell, Kathy. *Hearing Between the Lines: The Audience as Fellow Worker in Luke-Acts and its Literary Milieu*. LNTS 425. London: T. & T. Clark, 2010.

McCord Adams, Marilyn. "The Role of Miracles in the Structure of Luke-Acts." Pages 235–73 in *Hermes and Athena*. Edited by Eleonore Stump and Thomas P. Flint. Notre Dame, Indiana: University of Notre Dame Press, 1993.

McQueen, Larry R. *Joel and the Spirit: The Cry of a Prophetic Hermeneutic*. JPTSup 8. Sheffield: Sheffield Academic Press, 1995.

Meeks, Wayne A. *The First Urban Christians: The Social World of the Apostle Paul*. 2nd ed. New Haven: Yale University Press, 2003.

Menzies, Robert P. "A Pentecostal Perspective on Signs and Wonders." *Pneuma* 17.2 (1995): 265–78.

———. "Acts 2:17–21: A Paradigm for Pentecostal Mission." *JPT* 17.2 (2008): 200–218.

———. *Empowered for Witness: The Spirit in Luke-Acts*. London: T. & T. Clark, 2004.

———. "Luke and the Spirit: A Reply to James Dunn." *JPT* 4 (1994): 115–38.

———. "Spirit and Power in Luke-Acts: A Response to Max Turner." *JSNT* 49 (1993): 11–20.

———. *The Development of Early Christian Pneumatology with special reference to Luke-Acts*. JSNTSup 54. Sheffield: Sheffield Academic Press, 1991.

Menzies, William W. "The Methodology of Pentecostal Theology: An Essay on Hermeneutics." Pages 1–15 in *Essays on Apostolic Themes*. Edited by Paul Elbert. Peabody, Mass.: Hendrickson, 1985.

Metzger, Bruce M. "Ancient Astrological Geography and Acts 2:9–11." Pages 123–33 in *Apostolic History and the Gospel: Biblical and Historical Essays Presented to F.F.Bruce*. Edited by W. Ward Gasque and Ralph P. Martin. Exeter: Paternoster, 1970.

———. *A Textual Commentary on the Greek New Testament*. 2nd ed. Stuttgart: Deutsche Bibelgesellschaft, 1994.

Miles, Gary B. and Gary Trompf. "Luke and Antiphon: The Theology of Acts 27–28 in the Light of Pagan Beliefs about Divine Retribution, Pollution and Shipwreck." *HTR* 69 (1976): 259–67.

Mills, Watson E, ed. *Speaking in Tongues: A Guide to Research on Glossolalia*. Grand Rapids: Eerdmans, 1986.

Moessner, David P. "Two Lords 'at the Right Hand'? The Psalms and an Intertextual Reading of Peter's Pentecost Speech (Acts 2:14–36)." Pages 215–32 in *Literary Studies in Luke-Acts: Essays in Honor of Joseph B. Tyson*. Edited by Richard P. Thompson and Thomas E. Phillips. Georgia: Mercer University Press, 1998.

Montague, George T. *Holy Spirit: Growth of a Biblical Tradition*. Peabody, MA.: Hendrickson, 1976.

Morris, Leon. *Spirit of the Living God*. London: Inter-Varsity Fellowship, 1961.

Moule, C.F.D, ed. *Miracles*. Cambridge Studies in their Philosophy and History. London: A.R.Mowbray and Co Ltd., 1965.

Nasrallah, Laura. "The Acts of the Apostles, Greek Cities, and Hadrian's Panhellion." *JBL* 127.3 (2008): 533–66.

Neirynck, F. "The Miracle Stories in the Acts of the Apostles." Pages 169–213 in *Les Actes Des Apôtres: Traditions, Rédaction, Théologie*. Edited by J. Kremer. Leuven: Leuven University Press, 1979.

O'Brien, Peter T. *Ephesians*. PNTC. Leicester: Apollos, 1999.

O'Reilly Leo. *Word and Sign in the Acts of the Apostles: A Study in Lucan Theology*. Rome: Editrice Pontifica Universita Gregoriana, 1987.

Osborne, Grant R. *The Hermeneutical Spiral: A Comprehensive Introduction to Biblical Interpretation*. Leicester: Inter-Varsity Press, 1997.

Oss, Douglas A. "A Pentecostal/Charismatic View." Pages 239–283 in *Are Miraculous Gifts for Today*. Edited by Wayne Grudem. Leicester: Inter-Varsity Press, 1996.

Padilla, Osvaldo. "Hellenistic paideia and Luke's Education: A Critique of Recent Approaches." *NTS* 55.4 (2009): 416–37.

Palmer Robertson, O. *The Final Word: A Biblical Response to the Case for Tongues and Prophecy Today*. Edinburgh: Banner of Truth, 1993.

Pao, David W. *Acts and the Isaianic New Exodus*. Grand Rapids: Baker Academic, 2000.

Parsons, Mikael C. "The Place of Jerusalem on the Lukan Landscape: An Exercise in Symbolic Cartography." Pages 155–71 in *Literary Studies in Luke-Acts: Essays in Honor of Joseph B. Tyson*. Edited by Richard P. Thompson and Thomas E. Phillips. Georgia: Mercer University Press, 1998.

Parsons, Mikael C. *Acts*. PCNT. Grand Rapids: Baker Academic, 2008.

Pelikan, Jaroslav. *Acts*. BTCB. Grand Rapids: Brazos, 2005.

Penney, John Michael. *The Missionary Emphasis of Lukan Pneumatology*. JPTSup. Sheffield: Sheffield Academic Press, 1997.

Pervo, Richard I. *Acts*. Hermeneia. Minneapolis: Fortress Press, 2009.

———. *Profit with Delight*. Philadelphia: Fortress, 1987.

———. *The Mystery of Acts: Unravelling Its Story*. Santa Rosa: Polebridge, 2008.

Peterson, David G. "The Motif of Fulfilment and the Purpose of Luke-Acts." Pages 83–104 in BAIIFCS. Edited by Bruce W. Winter and Andrew D. Clarke. Grand Rapids: Eerdmans, 1993.

———. *The Acts of the Apostles*. PNTC. Nottingham: Apollos, 2009.

Petts, David. "The Baptism in the Holy Spirit: The Theological Distinctive." Pages 98–119 in *Pentecostal Perspectives*. Edited by Keith Warrington. Carlisle: Paternoster, 1998.

Phillips, Thomas E., ed. *Acts and Ethics*. NTM 9. Sheffield: Sheffield Phoenix Press, 2005.

Philo. Translated by F.H. Colson et al. 10 vols. LCL. Cambridge: Harvard University Press, 1929–1962.

Polhill, John B. *Acts*. NAC. Nashville, Tenn.: Broadman, 1992.

Porter, Stanley E. and Thomas H. Olbricht, eds. *Rhetoric, Scripture & Theology: Essays from the 1994 Pretoria Conference*. JSNTSup 131. Sheffield: Sheffield Academic Press, 1996.

Poythress, Vern Sheridan, "Modern Spiritual Gifts as Analogous to Apostolic Gifts: Affirming Extraordinary Works of the Spirit within Cessationist Theology." *JETS* 39.1 (1996): 71–101.

———. "Linguistic and Sociological Analyses of Modern Tongues-Speaking: Their Contributions and Limitations." Pages 469–92 in *Speaking in Tongues*. Edited by Watson E. Mills. Grand Rapids: Eerdmans, 1986.

Puskas, Charles B. *The Conclusion of Luke-Acts: The Significance of Acts 28:16–31*. Eugene, Or.: Pickwick, 2009.

Ravens, David. *Luke and the Restoration of Israel*. JSNTSup 119. Sheffield: Sheffield Academic Press, 1995.

Read-Heimerdinger, Jenny. *The Bezan Text of Acts: A Contribution of Discourse Analysis to Textual Criticism*. JSNTSup 236. Sheffield: Sheffield Academic Press, 2002.

Reiling, J. and J.L. Swellengrebel. *A Translator's Handbook on the Gospel of Luke*. Leiden: Brill, 1971.

Remus, H. "Miracle." In *ABD* 4:865.

Rengstorf, K.H. "σημεῖον" In *TDNT* 7:229–30.

Richard, Earl. "Pentecost as a Recurrent Theme in Luke-Acts." Pages 133–49 in *New Views on Luke and Acts*. Edited by Earl Richard. Collegeville, Minn.: Liturgical Press, 1990.

Richard, Earl, ed. *New Views on Luke and Acts*. Collegeville, Minn.: Liturgical Press, 1990.

Rius-Camps, Josep and Jenny Read-Heimerdinger. *The Message of Acts in Codex Bezae*. Vol. 1 of *The Message of Acts in Codex Bezae*. JSNTSup 257. London: T. & T. Clark, 2004.

Robinson, Anthony B. and Robert W. Wall. *Called to be Church: The Book of Acts for a New Day*. Grand Rapids: Eerdmans, 2006.

Rodman Williams, J. *God, the World and Redemption*. Vol. 2 of *Renewal Theology: Systematic Theology from a Charismatic Perspective*. Grand Rapids: Academie Books, 1988.

Rollston, Christopher A., ed. *The Gospels According to Michael Goulder*. Harrisburg, Penn.: Trinity, 2002.

Ross Wagner, J., C. Kavin Rowe, and Katherine Grieb, eds. *The Word Leaps the Gap: Essays on Scripture and Theology in honor of Richard B. Hays*. Grand Rapids: Eerdmans, 2008.

Rothschild, Clare K. *Luke-Acts and the Rhetoric of History*. WUNT 175. Tubingen: Mohr Siebeck, 2004.

Rowe, C. Kavin. *Early Narrative Christology: The Lord in the Gospel of Luke*. BZNW 139. Berlin: Walter de Gruyter, 2006.

Ruthven, Jon. ""This is My Covenant With Them": Isaiah 59:19–21 as the Programmatic Prophecy of the New Covenant in the Acts of the Apostles (part II)." *JPT* 17.2 (2008): 219–37.

———. *On the Cessation of the Charismata: The Protestant Polemic on Postbiblical Miracles*. JPTSup 3. Sheffield: Sheffield Academic Press, 1993.

Samuel Storms, C. "A Third Wave View." Pages 175–223 in *Are Miraculous Gifts for Today*. Edited by Wayne Grudem. Leicester: Inter-Varsity Press, 1996.

Saucy, Robert L. "An Open But Cautious View." Pages 95–148 in *Are Miraculous Gifts for Today*. Edited by Wayne Grudem. Leicester: Inter-Varsity Press, 1996.

Schmidt, K.L. "ἀσφάλεια" in *TDNT* 1:506.
Schreiner, Thomas R. *New Testament Theology: Magnifying God in Christ.* Grand Rapids: Baker, 2008.
Schweizer, E. *The Holy Spirit.* Translated by R.H. Fuller. Philadelphia: Fortress, 1978.
———. "πνεῦμα." In *TDNT* 6:404–415.
Scott Spencer, F. *Journeying Through Acts.* Peabody, Mass.: Hendrickson, 2004.
———. "Out of Mind, Out of Voice: Slave-Girls and Prophetic Daughters in Luke-Acts." *BI* 7 (1999): 133–55.
———. "Wise Up Young Man: The Moral Vision of Saul and Other neanaskoi in Acts." Pages 34–48 in *Acts and Ethics.* Edited by Thomas E. Phillips. NTM 9. Sheffield: Sheffield Phoenix Press, 2005.
Scott, James M. "Luke's Geographical Horizon." Pages 483–544 in *Graeco-Roman Setting.* Edited by David W.J. Gill and Conrad Gempf. BAIIFCS. Vol 2. Grand Rapids: Eerdmans, 1994.
Sheeley, Steven M. *Narrative Asides in Luke-Acts.* JSNTSup 72. Sheffield: JSOT Press, 1992.
Shepherd Jr., William H. *The Narrative Function of the Holy Spirit as a Character in Luke-Acts.* SBLDS 147. Atlanta, Georgia: Scholars Press, 1994.
Sleeman, Matthew. *Geography and the Ascension Narrative in Acts.* SNTSMS 146. Cambridge: Cambridge University Press, 2009.
Sloan, Robert. "'Signs and Wonders': A Rhetorical Clue to the Pentecost Discourse." *EQ* 63.3 (1991): 225–40.
Son, Sang-Won, ed. *History and Exegesis.* London: T & T Clark, 2006.
Sproul, R.C. *The Last Days According to Jesus.* Grand Rapids: Baker, 1998.
Stansell, Gary. *Micah and Isaiah: A Form and Tradition Historical Comparison.* SBLDS 85; Atlanta, Ga.: Scholar, 1988.
Stec, David M. *The Targum of Psalms.* Vol. 16 of *The Aramaic Bible.* London: T. & T. Clark, 2004.
Sternberg, Meier. *The Poetics of Biblical Narrative: Ideological Literature and the Drama of Reading.* Bloomington: Indiana University Press, 1987.
Stott, John R.W. *The Message of Acts.* BST. Leicester: Inter-Varsity Press, 1990.
———. *Baptism & Fullness: The Work of the Holy Spirit Today.* 2nd ed. Downers Grove, IL.: IVP, 1975.
Strauss, Mark L. *The Davidic Messiah in Luke-Acts.* JSNTSup 110. Sheffield: Sheffield Academic Press, 1995.
Stronstad, Roger. *The Charismatic Theology of St. Luke.* Peabody, Mass.: Hendrickson, 1984.
Stuart, Douglas. *Hosea-Jonah.* WBC 31. Waco, Tex.: Word, 1987.

Stump, Eleonore and Thomas P. Flint, eds. *Hermes and Athena*. Notre Dame, Indiana: University of Notre Dame Press, 1993.

Talbert, Charles H. *Reading Acts: A Literary and Theological Commentary on The Acts of the Apostles*. NY.: Crossroad, 1997.

Tannehill, Robert C. *The Narrative Unity of Luke-Acts: A Literary Interpretation. Volume 2: The Acts of the Apostles*. Minneapolis: Fortress, 1994.

———. *The Shape of Luke's Story: Essays on Luke-Acts*. Eugene, Or.: Cascade Books, 2005.

Thielman, Frank. *Ephesians*. BECNT. Grand Rapids: Baker, 2010.

Thiselton, Anthony C. *New Horizons in Hermeneutics: The Theory and Practice of Transforming Biblical Reading*. Grand Rapids: Zondervan, 1992.

———. *The Two Horizons: New Testament Hermeneutics and philosophical description with special reference to Heidegger, Bultmann, Gadamer and Wittgenstein*. Grand Rapids: Eerdmans, 1980.

———. *The First Epistle to the Corinthians*. NIGTC. Grand Rapids: Eerdmans, 2000.

———. *Hermeneutics: An Introduction*. Grand Rapids: Eerdmans, 2009.

Thompson, Alan J. *One Lord, One People: The Unity of the Church in Acts in its Literary Setting*. LNTS. London: T. & T. Clark, 2008.

Thompson, Richard P. and Thomas E. Phillips, eds. *Literary Studies in Luke-Acts: Essays in Honor of Joseph B. Tyson*. Georgia: Mercer University Press, 1998.

Thornton, L.S. *Confirmation: Its Place in the Baptismal Mystery*. London: A&C Black, 1954.

Tibbert, Steve, with Val Taylor. *Good to Grow: Building a Missional Church in the 21st Century – One Church's Story*. Milton Keynes: Authentic, 2011.

Tiede, David L. *Prophecy and History in Luke-Acts*. Philadelphia: Fortress Press, 1980.

Treier, Daniel J. "The Fulfilment of Joel 2:28-32: A Multiple-Lens Approach." *JETS* 40 (1:1997): 13-26.

Trites, Allison A. *The New Testament Concept of Witness*. SNTSMS 31. Cambridge: Cambridge University Press, 1977.

Turner, Max. "'Empowerment for Mission?' The Pneumatology of Luke-Acts: An Appreciation and Critique of James B. Shelton's Mighty in Word and Deed." *VE* 24 (1994): 103-121.

———. *Power from on High: The Spirit in Israel's Restoration and Witness in Luke-Acts*. Sheffield: Sheffield Academic Press, 1996.

———. "The 'Spirit of Prophecy' as the Power of Israel's Restoration and Witness." Pages 327-48 in *Witness to the Gospel*. Edited by I. Howard Marshall and David Peterson. Grand Rapids, Mi.: Eerdmans, 1998.

―――. *The Holy Spirit and Spiritual Gifts Then and Now*. Carlisle: Paternoster Press, 1996.

―――. "The Spirit and the Power of Jesus' Miracles in the Lucan Conception." *NovT* 33.2 (1991): 124–152.

Twelftree, Graham H. *People of the Spirit: Exploring Luke's View of Church*. London: SPCK, 2009.

Tyson, Joseph B. *Images of Judaism in Luke-Acts*. Columbia: University of South Carolina Press, 1992.

VanGemeren, Willem A. "The Spirit of Restoration." *WTJ* 50 (1988): 81–102.

Verheyden, J., ed. *The Unity of Luke-Acts*. Leuven: Leuven University Press, 1999.

Verhoef, P. "Prophecy" Pages 1067–1078 in vol. 4 of *NIDOTTE*. 5 vols. Grand Rapids: Zondervan, 1997.

Vermes, Geza. *The Dead Sea Scrolls: Qumran in Perspective*. London: Collins, 1977.

Virgil. *Aeneid*. 3 vols. Bibliotheca Classica. London: Whittaker & Co, 1871.

Wagner, C. Peter. *The Third Wave of the Holy Spirit: Encountering the Power of Signs and Wonders Today*. AnnArbor: Vine, 1988.

Wall, Robert W. "Acts." Pages 1–368 in *Acts, Romans, 1 Corinthians*. Edited by Leander Keck. Vol. X of *The New Interpreter's Bible*. Edited by Leander Keck. Nashville, Tenn.: Abingdon, 2002.

―――. "Israel and the Gentile Mission in Acts and Paul: A Canonical Approach." In *Witness to the Gospel*. Edited by I. Howard Marshall and David Peterson. Grand Rapids: Eerdmans, 1998.

Wallace, Daniel B. *Greek Grammar Beyond the Basics: An Exegetical Syntax of the New Testament*. Grand Rapids: Zondervan, 1996.

Walters, Patricia. *The Assumed Authorial Unity of Luke and Acts: A Reassessment of the Evidence*. SNTSMS 145. Cambridge: Cambridge University Press, 2009.

Walton, Steve. "Where Does the Beginning of Acts End?" Pages 447–67 in *The Unity of Luke-Acts*. Edited by J. Verheyden. Leuven: Leuven University Press, 1999.

Warfield, B.B. *Counterfeit Miracles*. Edinburgh: Banner of Truth, repr. 1995.

Warrington, Keith, ed. *Pentecostal Perspectives*. Carlisle: Paternoster, 1998.

Weatherly, Jon A. *Jewish Responsibility for the Death of Jesus in Luke-Acts*. JSNTSup 106. Sheffield: Sheffield Academic Press, 1994.

Wenk, Matthias. *Community-Forming Power: The Socio-Ethical Role of the Spirit in Luke-Acts*. JPTSup 19. Sheffield: Sheffield Academic Press, 2000.

Witherington, III, Ben. *The Acts of the Apostles: A Socio-Rhetorical Commentary*. Grand Rapids: Eerdmans, 1998.

———. "Salvation and Health in Christian Antiquity: The Soteriology of Luke-Acts in its First Century Setting." Pages 145–66 in *Witness to the Gospel*. Edited by I. Howard Marshall and David Peterson. Grand Rapids: Eerdmans, 1998.

Witherup, R.D. "Cornelius Over and Over and Over Again: 'Functional Redundancy' in the Acts of the Apostles." *JSNT* 43 (1993): 45–66.

———. "Functional Redundancy in the Acts of the Apostles: A Case Study." *JSNT* 48 (1992): 67–86.

Wolff, Hans Walter. *Joel and Amos*. Hermeneia. Philadelphia: Fortress, 1977.

Woodhouse, John. "Signs and Wonders and Evangelical Ministry." Pages 7–71 in *Signs and Wonders and Evangelicals*. Edited by R. Doyle. Randburg: Fabel, 1987.

Wright, N.T. *The New Testament and the People of God*. London: SPCK, 1993.

———. *Jesus and the Victory of God*. London: SPCK, 1996.

———. *Surprised by Hope*. London: SPCK, 2007.

Yamada, Kota. "A Rhetorical History: The Literary Genre of the Acts of the Apostles." Pages 230–50 in *Rhetoric, Scripture & Theology: Essays from the 1994 Pretoria Conference*. Edited by Stanley E. Porter and Thomas H. Olbricht. JSNTSup 131. Sheffield: Sheffield Academic Press, 1996.

Zehnle, Richard F. *Peter's Pentecost Discourse: Tradition and Lukan Reinterpretation in Peter's Speeches of Acts 2 and 3*. SBLMS 15. Nashville, Tenn.: Abingdon, 1971.

Zerhusen, Bob. "An Overlooked Diglossia in Acts 2." *BTB* 25 (1995): 118–30.

Zwiep, Arie W. *Judas and the Choice of Matthias*. Tubingen: Mohr Siebeck, 2004.

———. "Luke's Understanding of Baptism in the Holy Spirit." *PentecoStudies* 6:2 (2007): 127–49.

———. *The Ascension of the Messiah in Lukan Christology*. NovTSup 87. Leiden: Brill, 1997.

www.ingramcontent.com/pod-product-compliance
Lightning Source LLC
Chambersburg PA
CBHW071447160426
43195CB00013B/2047